# Contents

# 2 Heating or Reheating Chart

**1.** Directions below are for reheating already-cooked foods at refrigerator or room temperature. Use microwave oven safe containers.
**2.** Cover most foods (see tips) for fastest heating. Exceptions are rare or medium meats, some sandwiches, griddle foods like pancakes and baked foods.
**3.** Where appropriate, use the automatic food temperature probe for accurate heating. Place probe horizontally so tip is in center of food. Bubbling around edges of dish is normal, since center is last to heat. Suggested serving temperatures are given for most foods. Young children usually prefer cooler food, generally about 20° lower. Adjust temperatures to your personal taste. Stir foods before serving.
**4.** Be sure foods are heated through before serving. Steaming or bubbling around edges does not necessarily mean food is heated throughout. Stir food once or twice during heating, if possible, to ensure even thorough heating. As a general rule, hot foods produce an area warm to the touch in center of underside of dish.

| ITEM | Amount | Suggested Serving Temp. | Power Level | Approximate Time, Min. |
|---|---|---|---|---|
| **Appetizers** | | | | |
| Saucy: such as meatballs, riblets, cocktail | 1 to 2 servings | 150° | High | 2 to 4 |
| franks, etc. | 3 to 4 servings | 150° | High | 3 to 5 |
|   ½ cup serving | | | | |
| Dips: cream or process cheese | ½ cup | 130° | Medium | 2 to 3 |
| | 1 cup | 130° | Medium | 3 to 5 |
| Pastry bites: small pizzas, egg rolls, etc. | 2 to 4 servings | | High | 1 to 2½ |
| **Tip:** Cover saucy appetizers with wax paper. Cover dips with plastic wrap. Do not cover pastry bites, they will not be crisp. | | | | |
| **Plate of Leftovers** | | | | |
| Meat plus 2 vegetables | 1 plate | 150°-160° | High | 3 to 4 |
| **Tip:** Probe works well in saucy dishes or vegetables (use in largest serving) but not in meat slices. Cover plate of food with wax paper or plastic wrap. Rotate plate ½ turn after half of time. | | | | |
| **Meats and Main Dishes** | | | | |
| Saucy main dishes: chop suey, spaghetti, | 1 to 2 servings | 150°-160° | High | 4 to 10 |
| creamed chicken, chili, stew, macaroni and | 3 to 4 servings | 150°-160° | High | 10 to 13 |
| cheese, etc. | 1 can 16-oz. | 150°-160° | High | 5 to 7 |
|   ¾-1 cup/serving | | | | |
| Thinly sliced roasted meat: | | | | |
| Rare beef roast, minimum time: Medium rare, | 1 to 2 servings | | Med-High | 1 to 2 |
| maximum time | 3 to 4 servings | | Med-High | 2½ to 3½ |
|   3 to 4-oz./serving | | | | |
| Well done: beef, pork, ham, poultry, etc. | 1 to 2 servings | | Med-High | 1½ to 3 |
| | 3 to 4 servings | | Med-High | 4½ to 6 |
| Steaks, chops, ribs, other meat pieces: | | | | |
| Rare beef steak | 1 to 2 servings | 130° | Med-High | 1½ to 2½ |
| | 3 to 4 servings | 130° | Med-High | 3 to 5 |
| Well done beef, chops, ribs, etc. | 1 to 2 servings | 150° | Med-High | 2 to 3½ |
| | 3 to 4 servings | 150° | Med-High | 3 to 5 |
| Hamburgers or meat loaf | 1 to 2 servings | | High | 1½ to 2½ |
|   4-oz./serving | 3 to 4 servings | | High | 3½ to 4½ |
| Chicken pieces | 1 to 2 pieces | | High | 2½ to 3½ |
| | 3 to 4 pieces | | High | 5 to 7 |
| Hot dogs and sausages | 1 to 2 | | High | 1 to 1½ |
| | 3 to 4 | | High | 1½ to 2½ |
| Breakfast sausage links | 2 | | High | 1 to 1½ |
| | 4 | | High | 1½ to 2 |
| | 8 | | High | 2 to 2½ |
| Rice and pasta | 1 to 2 servings | 150° | High | 1 to 2½ |
|   ⅔-¾ cup/serving | | | | |
| Topped or mixed with sauce | 1 to 2 servings | 150°-160° | High | 3 to 5 |
|   ⅔-¾ cup/serving | 3 to 4 servings | 150°-160° | High | 5 to 8 |

**Tip:** Cover saucy main dishes with plastic wrap. Cover other main dishes and meats with wax paper. Do not cover rare or medium rare meats. When heating or reheating 3 or 4 servings of meat slices or pieces, rotate utensil ½ turn after half of time.

| ITEM | Amount | Suggested Serving Temp. | Power Level | Approximate Time, Min. |
|---|---|---|---|---|
| **Sandwiches & Soups** | | | | |
| Moist filling: Sloppy joe, barbecue, ham salad, | 1 to 2 servings | | Med-High | 1 to 2 |
| etc. in bun | 3 to 4 servings | | Med-High | 3 to 4 |
| ⅓ cup/serving | | | | |
| Thick meat-cheese filling: with firm bread | 1 to 2 servings | | Med-High | 2 to 3 |
| | 3 to 4 servings | | Med-High | 4 to 5 |
| Soup | | | | |
| Water based | 1 to 2 servings | 150°-170° | High | 2 to 6 |
| 1 cup/serving | 3 to 4 servings | 150°-170° | High | 7 to 11 |
| | 1 can 10-oz. reconstituted | 150°-170° | High | 7 to 8 |
| Milk based | 1 to 2 servings | 140° | Med-High | 4 to 7 |
| 1 cup/serving | 3 to 4 servings | 140° | Med-High | 10 to 13 |
| | 1 can 10-oz. reconstituted | 140° | Med-High | 8 to 9 |

**Tip:** Use paper towel or napkin to cover sandwiches. Cover soups with wax paper or plastic wrap.

| ITEM | Amount | Suggested Serving Temp. | Power Level | Approximate Time, Min. |
|---|---|---|---|---|
| **Vegetables** | | | | |
| Small pieces: peas, beans, corn, etc. | 1 to 2 servings | 150°-160° | High | ½ to 4 |
| ½ cup/serving | 3 to 4 servings | 150°-160° | High | 5 to 7 |
| | 1 can 16-oz. | 150°-160° | High | 4 to 5 |
| Large pieces or whole: asparagus spears, potato. | 1 to 2 servings | | High | 2 to 3 |
| | 3 to 4 servings | | High | 4 to 6 |
| | 1 can 16-oz. | | High | 4 to 6 |
| Corn on the cob | 1 to 2 ears | | High | 3 to 5 |
| | 3 to 4 ears | | High | 6 to 9 |
| Mashed potatoes | 1 to 2 servings | 150°-160° | High | 2½ to 4½ |
| ½ cup/serving | 3 to 4 servings | 150°-160° | High | 6 to 8 |

**Tip:** Cover vegetables for most even heating.

| ITEM | Amount | Suggested Serving Temp. | Power Level | Approximate Time, Min. |
|---|---|---|---|---|
| **Sauces** | | | | |
| Dessert: chocolate, butterscotch | ½ cup | 125° | High | 1 to 1½ |
| | 1 cup | 125° | High | 2 to 2½ |
| Meat or main dish, chunky type: giblet gravy, | ½ cup | 150°-160° | High | 2 to 3½ |
| spaghetti sauce, etc. | 1 cup | 150°-160° | High | 3 to 5 |
| | 1 can 16-oz. | 150°-160° | High | 4 to 6 |
| Creamy type | ½ cup | 140°-150° | High | 2 to 3 |
| | 1 cup | 140°-150° | High | 3½ to 4½ |

**Tip:** Cover food to prevent spatter.

| ITEM | Amount | Suggested Serving Temp. | Power Level | Approximate Time, Min. |
|---|---|---|---|---|
| **Bakery Foods** | | | | |
| Cake, coffee cake, doughnuts, sweet rolls, nut | 1 piece | | Low | ¼ to ½ |
| or fruit bread | 2 pieces | | Low | 1 to 1½ |
| | 4 pieces | | Low | 1½ to 2 |
| | 9-in. cake or 12 rolls or doughnuts | | Low | 2 to 4 |
| Dinner rolls, muffins | 1 | | Medium | ¼ to ½ |
| | 2 | | Medium | ½ to ¾ |
| | 4 | | Medium | ½ to 1 |
| | 6 to 8 | | Medium | 1 to 2 |
| Pie: fruit, nut or custard | 1 slice | | High | ½ to 1 |
| ⅛ of 9-in. pie=1 slice | 2 slices | | High | 1 to 1½ |
| (use minimum time for custard) | 4 slices | | Med-High | 2 to 3 |
| | 9-in. pie | | Med-High | 3 to 5 |

**Tip:** Do not cover.

| ITEM | Amount | Suggested Serving Temp. | Power Level | Approximate Time, Min. |
|---|---|---|---|---|
| **Griddle Foods** | | | | |
| Pancakes, French toast or waffles (3"×4") | | | | |
| Plain, no topping | 2 or 3 pieces | | High | 1 to 1½ |
| Syrup & butter | 2 or 3 pieces | | High | 1 to 1½ |
| With 2 sausage patties (cooked) | 2 or 3 pieces | | High | 1½ to 2 |

**Tip:** Do not cover.

| ITEM | Amount | Suggested Serving Temp. | Power Level | Approximate Time, Min. |
|---|---|---|---|---|
| **Beverages** | | | | |
| Coffee, tea, cider | 1 to 2 cups | 160°-170° | High | 2 to 4 |
| other water based | 3 to 4 cups | 160°-170° | High | 5 to 7 |
| Cocoa, other milk based | 1 to 2 cups | 140° | Med-High | 3 to 5 |
| | 3 to 4 cups | 140° | Med-High | 7½ to 10 |

**Tip:** Do not cover.

# 4 Defrosting Chart

**1.** Unwrap food. If it is difficult to remove plastic grocery store tray, it may be removed after first half of time. Place food on microwave safe trivet in microwave safe cooking dish.
**2.** After first half of cooking time, remove any remaining wrap. Break food apart or separate, if possible. Remove any thawed food, if possible. Shield bone tips, thin meat or warm areas of large pieces of food with foil.
**3.** Large bulky roasts may have icy center. Allow 15 to 45 minutes stand time. Poultry may be placed under running cool water until giblets can be removed.
**4.** When defrosted, food should be cool, but softened in all areas. If still slightly icy after second half of defrosting time, return to microwave oven very briefly, or let stand a few minutes.

## POWER LEVEL: Defrost

| FOOD | First Half Time, Min. | Second Half Time, Min. | Comments |
|---|---|---|---|
| **Meat** | | | |
| Bacon (12-16 oz. pkg.) | 2 | 1½ to 2 | Place unopened package on trivet in cooking dish in oven. Turn over after first half of time. Let stand 5 minutes. |
| Franks (1-lb.) | 3 | 2 | Place unopened package on trivet in cooking dish in oven. Microwave just until franks can be separated. Turn over after first 3 minutes. |
| Ground: beef & pork (1-lb.) (2-lb.) | 4<br>7 to 8 | 3 to 5<br>6 to 8 | Place unwrapped meat on trivet in cooking dish. Scrape off softened meat after each half of time. Set aside. After second half of time, break up remaining block, microwave 1 to 3 minutes more. |
| Roast: Boneless Beef, (up to 4-lb.)<br>Boneless Pork, (up to 3-lb.) | 5 per lb.<br>5 per lb. | 3 per lb.<br>3 to 4 per lb. | Place unwrapped meat on trivet in cooking dish in oven. After half of time, turn roast over and shield ends. Defrost for second half of time. Let stand for 30 minutes. |
| Roast, Bone in Pork, (up to 3-lb.) | 4 per lb. | 4 to 5 per lb. | Place unwrapped meat on trivet in cooking dish in oven. Shield ends of roast with foil for first half of time. Turn roast over and remove foil from ends. Shield top thin bones with foil during second half. Let stand 30 minutes. |
| Steaks, chops & cutlets: beef, lamb, pork & veal | 3 to 4 per lb. | 2 to 4 per lb. | Place unwrapped meat in single layer on trivet in cooking dish in oven. Turn over after first half of time. Remove any defrosted pieces. After second half of time, separate pieces with table knife. Let stand to complete defrosting. |
| Sausage, bulk (1-lb. tray)<br>(1-lb. roll) | 2 to 3<br>2 to 3 | 2½ to 4½<br>2 to 4 | Turn over after first half of time.<br>Turn over after first half of time and shield ends with foil. Turn over once during second half of time. |
| Sausage, link (½ to 1-lb.)<br>Sausage, patties (12-oz. pkg.) | 2<br>2 | 2 to 3<br>1 to 2 | Rearrange after first half of time.<br>Rotate patties after first half of time. |
| **Poultry** | | | |
| Chicken, broiler-fryer pieces, (1 to 1½-lb.) | 4 | 4 to 5 | Place unwrapped chicken in single layer on trivet in cooking dish in oven. Turn chicken over after half of time and separate pieces. After second half, remove defrosted pieces. Microwave 2 to 4 minutes more, if necessary. |
| Whole (2½ to 3½-lb.) | 12 | 10 to 11 | Place unwrapped chicken on trivet in cooking dish in oven. After first half of time, turn over chicken. Shield bone ends, wings, tail and warm areas with foil. |
| Cornish hen | 6 per lb. | 4 to 6 per lb. | Place hens breast-side up on trivet in cooking dish in oven. Turn over after first half of time. Rinse cavity to loosen giblets. |

POWER LEVEL: **Defrost**

| FOOD | First Half<br>Time, Min. | Second Half<br>Time, Min. | Comments |
|---|---|---|---|
| **Fish & Seafood** | | | |
| Fillets (1-lb.) | 4 | 4 to 5 | Place unwrapped fish on trivet in dish. Turn over after first |
| Steaks (6-16 oz.) | 2 to 3 | 2 to 3 | half of time, shield ends with foil. After second half of time, |
| Steaks (1-2 lb.) | 4 to 5 | 3 to 5 | hold under cold water to separate. |
| Whole fish (8 to 10-oz.) | 3 | 2 to 4 | Place fish in cooking dish. Turn over after first half of time and shield tail section with foil. After second half of time, rinse cavity with cold water to complete defrosting. |
| Shellfish, small pieces (1-lb.) | 4 | 3 to 5 | Spread shellfish in single layer in cooking dish. Break up after 5 minutes. Let stand 5 minutes. |
| Shellfish, blocks, Crab meat (6-oz. pkg.) | 3 | 2 | Place block in casserole. Turn over after first half of time. |
| Oysters (8 to 12-oz. container) | 3 | 2 to 3 | Place block in casserole. Break up with fork after first half of time. |
| Scallops (1-lb. pkg.) | 5 | 3 | Place unwrapped scallops on trivet in cooking dish in oven. Turn over and separate after first half of time. |
| Shellfish, Large | 4 to 5 | 2 to 4 | Arrange on trivet in cooking dish. Turn over after first half of time. |
| Crab legs—1 to 2 (8 to 10-oz.) | 4 to 5 | none | Arrange on trivet in cooking dish. |
| Lobster tails—1 to 2 (6 to 9-oz.) | 4 to 5 | none | Arrange on trivet in cooking dish. |
| Whole lobster or crab (1½-lb ) | 5 to 6 | 3 to 4 | Place in cooking dish with darker side up. Turn over after first half of time. |
| **Breads, Cakes** | | | |
| Bread or buns (1-lb.) | 4 to 6 | none | |
| Heat & serve rolls (7-oz. pkg.) | 2½ to 4½ | none | |
| Coffee Cake (11 to 14¾-oz.) | 3½ to 5 | none | |
| Coffee ring (10-oz. pkg.) | 3½ to 5 | none | |
| Sweet rolls (8¾ to 12-oz.) | 4 to 6 | none | |
| Doughnuts (1 to 4) | 1½ to 3 | none | |
| Doughnuts, glazed (1 box of 8 large) | 4 to 6 | none | |
| French Toast (2 slices) | 4 to 5 | none | |
| Cake, Bundt type (24-oz.) | 5 to 6 | none | Let stand 10 to 30 minutes. |
| Cake, frosted 2 to 3 layer (17-oz.) | 2 to 4 | none | Let stand 10 to 20 minutes. |
| Cake, filled or topped 1 layer (12½ to 16-oz.) | 2 to 4 | none | Remove from foil pan if necessary. Let stand 10 minutes. |
| Pound cake (10¾-oz.) | 2 to 4 | none | Remove from foil pan if necessary. Let stand 10 minutes. |
| Cheesecake, plain or fruit top (17 to 19-oz.) | 5 to 7 | none | Remove from foil pan if necessary. Let stand 20 to 30 minutes. |
| Crunch cakes & cupcakes | ½ to 1½ each | none | |
| Fruit or nut pie (8-in.) | 8 to 15 | none | Let stand 20 to 30 minutes. |
| Cream or custard pie (14 to 23-oz.) | 8 to 12 | none | Let stand 20 to 30 minutes. |
| **Fruit** | | | |
| Fresh (10 to 16-oz.) | 7 to 10 | none | Remove foil or metal. Place package in oven. After minimum time, break up with fork. Repeat if necessary. |
| Plastic pouch (10-oz. pkg.) | 4 to 5 | none | Place package in oven. Flex package once. |

# 6 Convenience Food Chart

**1.** Most convenience foods can be reheated by microwave only, since they are already cooked. Always use microwave safe utensils (glass or plastic). For foods needing browning or crisping, conventional baking is recommended.
**2.** Remove food from foil containers over ¾-in. high.

| FOOD | Container | Cover | Power Level & Time | | Comments |
|---|---|---|---|---|---|
| **Appetizers & Snacks** | | | | | |
| Pastry Bites | Microwave safe dish | No | High | 2 to 4 min. | Place on trivet in dish. |
| Frozen prepared Sandwiches | Paper towel | No | High | 2 to 2½ min. per sandwich | Remove from package pouch and wrap in paper towel. Rotate ½ turn after half of time. |
| Frozen Egg or Pizza Rolls (6½-oz. pkg.) | Microwave safe dish | No | High | 3½ to 4½ min. | Place on trivet in microwave safe dish. |
| Canned sausage (5-oz. can) | Microwave safe dish | Wax paper | High | 3 to 4 min. | Drain and cut into bite-size pieces. Add ½ cup chili or cocktail sauce. |
| Fish sticks (6 to 8-oz.) | Microwave safe dish | No | High | 4½ to 7 min. | Place on trivet in dish. |
| Pizza, frozen (individual size) | Microwave safe dish | No | Med-High | 2 to 2½ min. per slice | Place on trivet in dish. |
| **Eggs & Cheese** | | | | | |
| Scrambled egg substitute (8½-oz. carton) | Microwave safe dish | No | Defrost | 5 to 6 min. | To Defrost: Defrost in carton 4 minutes. Pour into casserole. Break up ice and defrost 2 minutes longer. |
| | | | Med-High | 3 to 4 min. | To Cook: Stir after 2 minutes, then every minute until desired firmness. |
| Cheese souffle (12-oz. pkg.) | Microwave safe pie plate and custard cups | No | Defrost | 7 to 10 min. | To Defrost: Place in pie plate. Stir twice. |
| | | | Med-High | 6 to 7 min. | To Cook: Divide between 3 or 4 buttered custard cups, 6 to 7-oz. Rearrange after 5 minutes. Souffles are done when center is almost set. |
| Scrambled eggs breakfast (6¼-oz.) with sausage and hash brown potatoes | Package paper tray | Pkg. cover | Med-High | 4 to 6 min. | Remove paper tray from carton, turn back clear film to expose potatoes. |
| **Fish & Shellfish** | | | | | |
| Crab shrimp or lobster newburg (6½-oz.) | Package pouch | No | High | 4 to 5 min. | Place pouch in microwave safe dish. Puncture pouch with fork to vent. Stir before serving. |
| Fish & chips (5 to 14-oz.) | Package tray or Microwave safe dish | No | High | 4 to 7 min. | Distribute evenly on trivet in microwave safe dish. |
| Deviled crab cakes (6-oz.) | Microwave safe dish | No | High | 2½ to 4 min. | Distribute evenly on trivet in microwave safe dish. Rearrange after half time. |
| Breaded fish (5 to 10-oz.) | Microwave safe dish | No | High | 4 to 7 min. | Distribute evenly on trivet in microwave safe dish, or line with paper towels. Rearrange after half time. |
| **Meat** | | | | | |
| Frozen meats (5 to 8-oz.) (10 to 16-oz.) | Microwave safe dish or pouch | Lid or plastic wrap. Do not cover pouch. | High | 4 to 9 min. 8 to 18 min. | Stir meat pieces and spoon sauce over after half time. If pouch package is used, puncture with fork to vent. Do not cover pouch. |
| Dry mixes (hamburger added) | Microwave safe casserole | Lid | High | 11 to 15 min. | Add cooked, drained hamburger. Stir after 7 minutes. |
| T.V. dinners (6 to 8-oz.) (8½ to 12-oz.) | Package tray and carton | Carton or plastic wrap | Med-High | 7 to 9 min. 8 to 12 min. | Remove foil cover. Remove brownie or cobbler dessert to custard cup, cover and microwave on Medium High 1½ to 3 minutes. Replace dinner in carton or cover with plastic wrap. |
| **Pasta, Rice** | | | | | |
| Canned spaghetti, etc. (16-oz.) | Microwave safe dish | Lid or plastic wrap | High | 4 to 6 min. | Stir before serving. |
| Frozen rice in pouch (10-oz.) | Pouch | No | High | 8 to 10 min. | Place pouch in microwave safe dish. Puncture pouch with fork to vent. Stir before serving. |
| Frozen macaroni & cheese, spaghetti (8 to 14-oz.) (20-oz.) | Microwave safe dish | Lid or plastic wrap | Med-High | 9 to 15 min. 16 to 18 min. | Stir before serving. |
| Frozen Lasagna (10½-oz.) (21-oz.) | Microwave safe dish | Lid or plastic wrap | Medium Medium | 16 to 19 min. 25 to 28 min. | Rotate after 15 minutes. Let stand 5 minutes before serving. |

| FOOD | Container | Cover | Power Level & Time | | Comments |
|---|---|---|---|---|---|
| **Poultry** | | | | | |
| Canned (5 to 10½-oz.) (14 to 24-oz.) | Microwave safe dish | Lid or plastic wrap | High High | 2 to 3½ min. 4 to 6 min. | Place in microwave safe dish. Cover; stir after half time. |
| Frozen Pouch (5 to 6½-oz.) | Pouch | No | High | 4 to 6 min. | Place pouch in microwave safe dish. Slit pouch before microwaving. |
| Frozen Main Dish (12-oz. pkg.) | Microwave safe dish | No | Med-High | 7 to 8 min. | Stir or rotate after 5 minutes. |
| Frozen Fried Chicken 2-pieces 1-lb., 4 to 6 pieces | Microwave safe dish | No | High | 5 to 6 min. 9 to 10 min. | If label does not state "fully cooked", check for doneness. |
| **Sauces, Gravies** | | | | | |
| Canned (10 to 16-oz.) | Microwave safe dish | Lid or plastic wrap | High | 4 to 5 min. | Stir after half time. |
| **Vegetables** | | | | | |
| Frozen breaded (7 to 8 oz.) | Microwave safe dish | No | High | 4 to 6 min. | Place on microwave trivet in dish. |
| Canned (8 to 9-oz.) (15 to 17-oz.) (28 to 32-oz.) | Microwave safe dish | Lid or plastic warp | High | 2½ to 3½ min. 4 to 5½ min. 6½ to 8 min. | Place undrained vegetables in microwave safe dish. Cover. (Or use temperature probe set to 150°.) |
| Instant mashed potatoes (2 to 6 servings) | Microwave safe dish | Lid or plastic wrap | High | 2½ to 7 min. | Follow package instructions. Cover. After heating, briskly stir in potatoes, adding extra 1 to 2 tablespoons dry mix. Heat 1 to 2 minutes. |
| Frozen souffle (12-oz. pkg.) | Microwave safe pie plate and custard cups | No | Defrost Med-High | 7 to 10 min. 6 to 7 min. | To Defrost: Place souffle in pie plate. To Cook: Divide between 4 custard cups. Souffles are done when centers are almost set. |
| Potatoes: baked, stuffed, frozen 1 to 2 3 to 4 | Microwave safe dish on trivet | Wax paper | High High | 7 to 13 min. 16 to 22 min. | Remove any foil. |

## Freezer to Table Home Frozen Foods Chart

| FOOD | Amount | Defrost Time | Hold Time | Power Level & Time | | Comments |
|---|---|---|---|---|---|---|
| Meatballs, raw | 1 recipe (12) | 10 | 5 | High | 7 to 9 min. | Arrange in circle, cover with plastic wrap. Rotate ½ turn after half time. For precooked meatballs reduce each time period by 2 minutes. |
| Meat loaf, raw | 1 recipe (round loaf) 9×5-in. loaf | 30 30 | 15 15 | Med-High Medium | 25 to 30 min. 30 to 35 min. | Cover with plastic wrap. If precooked, add ½ cup water and reduce cook time period by 10 minutes. Shield ends of loaf with foil until last 15 minutes. Rotate ¼ turn every 10 minutes. |
| Saucy casseroles (Chicken a la King, chili, spaghetti sauce, beef stew) | 1 recipe (1½-qt.) 1 cup (8-oz.) | 30 to 35 8 to 10 | none 5 | Med-High Med-High | 15 to 18 min. 4 to 5 min. | Cover with plastic wrap. Freeze food in flat casseroles for fastest heating. |
| Soup | 2-qt. 1-qt. | 30 25 | 20 15 | Med-High Med-High | 25 to 30 min. 15 to 18 min. | Cover. Break up and stir while defrosting and cooking, to speed heating. |

# 8 Meats

1. Always use microwave-safe dish, plastic or glass.
2. See chart below for specific instructions. After two-thirds of cooking time or when temp probe reaches 90°, turn meat over. Shield any bone tips, thin meat areas or portions that are starting to overcook with foil.
3. Standing time: Allow about 10 minutes standing time for most roasts before carving.

| FOOD | Container | Cover | Power Level & Time (or Internal Temp.) | | Comments |
|---|---|---|---|---|---|
| **BEEF** | | | | | |
| Ground Crumbled (for casseroles or soup) | Casserole | No | High | 1lb.. 6 to 8 min.<br><br>1½ lb.:<br>9 to 11 min. | Stir every 2 minutes. Add sauce or casserole ingredients and finish. To cook frozen block, microwave 12 to 15 minutes breaking up and stirring every 5 minutes. |
| Meatballs | Pie plate or 8-in. round dish | Wax paper | High | 1 lb.:<br>9 to 10 min. | Arrange around edge of dish. Rotate dish ¼ turn after half time. |
| Patties | 8-in. square glass dish (with trivet if desired), or ceramic dinner plate (For 1 to 2 patties use paper plate lined with double thickness paper towels.) | Wax paper | High | 4 patties/lb.<br><br>1 to 2 patties:<br>2½ to 4 min.<br><br>3 to 4 patties:<br>5½ to 7 min. | If desired, add browning sauce or agent. Let patties stand, covered, 2 minutes. |
| Meat Loaf | Pie plate or loaf dish | Plastic wrap | High<br><br>Med-High or cook to 170° | Round loaf:<br>22 to 25 min.<br><br>Loaf shape:<br>30 to 35 min. | Let stand 10 minutes after cooking.<br><br>Shield ends of loaf with foil to prevent over cooking during last 15 min.. |
| **ROASTS** | | | | | |
| Pot roasts (up to 3-lbs.) | 2-qt. casserole or 8-in. square dish | Lid or wax paper | High, then<br><br>Low | 10 min.<br><br>25 to 30 min./lb | Brush with browning sauce and add ½ cup water per lb. meat. Cover with lid or wax paper. Turn over after half of time. Add vegetables if desired after half of time. Recover and finish. |
| Tender roasts (rib, high quality rump, sirloin tip) (up to 3-lbs.) | 8-in. square dish and trivet | Wax paper | Medium<br><br>  Min. per lb.  Internal Temp.<br>Rare 12 to 14 115° to 125°<br>Medium 14 to 16 125° to 140°<br>Well 17 to 19 140° to 155° | | Start meat fat or cut side down. Temperature probe cooking yields most accurate results. Let meat stand 10 to 15 minutes before carving. If desired, brush with browning sauce or agent before cooking. |
| Veal, shoulder, boneless (up to 3-lbs.) | 8-in. square dish and trivet | Wax paper | Medium | 16 to 17½ min. per lb. | Turn over after half of time. |
| Lamb, bone in, shank half (3-lbs.) | 8-in. square dish and trivet | Wax paper | Medium<br><br>  Min. per lb.  Internal Temp.<br>Medium 10½ to 12 130°<br>Well done 16 to 17 170° | | Turn over after half of time. Shield end of shank bone with foil during first half of time. |
| Boneless (up to 3-lbs.) | 8-in. square dish | Wax paper | Medium<br><br>  Min. per lb.  Internal Temp.<br>Medium 12 130°<br>Well done 16 to 17 170° | | Turn over after half of time. Shield smaller end of roast with foil during last half of cooking. |

| FOOD | Container | Cover | Power Level & Time (or Internal Temp.) | | Comments |
|---|---|---|---|---|---|
| **PORK** | | | | | |
| Bacon | Microwave safe plate | Paper towel | High | ¾ to 1 min. per slice | Arrange in single layer on paper towels or on trivet set in dish. |
| Pork sausage patties (raw) | Microwave safe utensil | Wax paper | High | ½ lb.: 4 patties 4½ to 5 min. | Arrange in single layer. Rearrange after half time. |
| Pork link sausage (raw) | Microwave safe utensil | Wax paper | High | ½ to ¾ min. per link | Arrange in single layer. Rearrange after half time. |
| Canadian bacon | Microwave safe utensil | Wax paper | High | 2 slices ½ to ¾ min. 4 slices 1 to 1¼ min. 6 slices 1½ to 2 min. | Arrange in single layer. |
| Pork chops | Microwave safe dinner plate, or 8-in. square dish | Plastic wrap | Medium | 2—(½ to ¾ lb.) 8 to 10 min. 3—(¾ to 1 lb.) 10 to 13 min. 4—(1 to 1¼ lb.) 14 to 18 min. | Brush with barbecue sauce or browning agent, if desired. Let stand covered 5 to 10 minutes before serving. Rotate dish ½ turn after half time. |
| Pork roast (up to 3-lb | Microwave safe 8 in square dish on trivet | Cooking bag | Low | 20 to 24 min. per lb. Or microwave to 170° Internal temp. | Tie end of bag securely. Do not use metal twist ties. |
| Canned Ham (3-lb.) | 8-in. square dish | Plastic wrap | Medium | 10 to 12 min. per lb. | Tie ham. Shield around top cut edges with 1-inch strip of foil. Place on trivet. Rotate after half time. Let stand 10 minutes. |
| Shank or Butt half Fully cooked (up to 3-lb.) | 8-in. square dish | Plastic wrap | Medium | 13 to 15 min. per lb. | Shield edge of ham with 1-in. wide strip of foil. Add ¼ cup water and cover. If using probe, microwave to 115°F internal temp. Let stand 5 to 10 minutes before carving. |
| Ham loaf | 6-cup ring mold | Plastic wrap | Medium | 18 to 23 min. (or microwave to internal temp. of 170°) | Let stand 5 minutes before serving. If a glaze is desired, spoon pineapple or apricot preserves over cooked ham loaf a few minutes before serving. |
| Ham slices & steaks (up to 3-lb.) | 8-in. square dish | Wax paper | Medium | 10 to 12 min. per lb. | Turn over at half time. |
| Lamb, Veal Chops & cutlets 1–2 3–4 | Brown'n sear dish | No | High | 6 to 8 min. per lb. 7 to 9 min. per lb. | Preheat Brown'n sear dish 6 to 8 minutes. Turn chop/cutlet over after 3 minutes. |

# 10 Poultry

1. Use microwave trivet for chicken and other small poultry.
2. Let chicken and other small poultry stand after microwaving for up to 10 minutes.

| FOOD | Container | Cover | Power Level & Time (or Internal Temp.) | | Comments |
|---|---|---|---|---|---|
| **CHICKEN** | | | | | |
| Pieces | Plate or 8-in. square dish | Wax paper | High | 4 to 6 min. per piece | Brush with browning sauce if desired. Arrange in single layer in cooking dish so thickest meaty pieces are near edges of dish. |
| Whole Unstuffed 4 to 5 lbs. | 8-Inch square dish with trivet | Oven-proof cooking bag or wax paper | Med-High | 12 to 14 min. per lb. | Brush with browning sauce if desired. Add ⅓ cup water to cooking bag. Slit bag near closure to vent. Do not use metal tie on bag. Cook breast side up. Or, place chicken breast down on trivet in dish and cover with wax paper. Microwave at Med-High, turning over and recovering after half of time. |
| 2 to 4 lbs. | 8-inch square dish with trivet | | High (or cook to 190° internal temp.) | 8 to 10 min. per lb. | |
| Stuffed | 8-inch square dish with trivet | Wax paper | Med-High (or cook to 190° internal temp.) | 16 to 19 min. per lb. | |
| **CORNISH HENS** | | | | | |
| Whole (stuffed or unstuffed) | 8-in. square dish and trivet | Wax paper | High | 8½ to 10 min. per lb. | Place breast side down in dish. Turn over after two-thrids of time. |
| Halves | 8-in. square dish | Wax paper | High | 9½ to 10½ min. per lb. | Arrange skin side up in dish, on bed of stuffing, if desired. |
| **TURKEY BREAST** (3 to 4 lbs.) | 8-in. square dish and trivet | Wax paper | Med-High (or cook to 170° internal temp.) | 15 to 17 min. per lb. | Brush with butter and browning sauce. |

# Fish

1. Fish is done when it flakes easily with a fork. Center may still be slightly transluscent, but will continue cooking as fish stands a few minutes after cooking.
2. Cook fish with or without sauce. A tight cover steams fish, or use a lighter cover of wax paper or paper towel for less steaming.
3. Do not overcook fish. Check at minimum time.

| FOOD | Container | Cover | Power Level & Time (or Internal Temp.) | | Comments |
|---|---|---|---|---|---|
| **FISH** | | | | | |
| Fillets or steaks 1-lb. | 8-in. square dish | Wax paper or plastic wrap | High | 7 to 8½ min. | Microwave until fish flakes easily. Let stand 3 minutes before serving. |
| Whole fish | 8-in. square dish | Plastic wrap | High | 5 to 7 min. per lb. Temp. (150°) | Shield head and thin tail with aluminum foil. Let stand 3 minutes before serving. |
| Oysters Clams, 6 | Pie plate or shallow dish | Plastic wrap | High | 3 to 4 min. | Arrange in circle. |
| Shrimp—1 lb. (peeled) | Pie plate or shallow dish | Plastic wrap | High | 5 to 6 min. | Stir once during cooking. |
| Shrimp (unpeeled) 1-lb. | 2-qt. casserole | Lid or plastic wrap | High | 5½ to 7 min. | Stir twice during cooking. |

# Eggs and Cheese

1. Prepare eggs many ways in the microwave oven, see below. Always pierce whole yolks before microwaving to prevent bursting.
2. Never hard cook eggs in the shell, and do not reheat in-shell hard cooked eggs. They could explode.
3. Cook eggs just until set, they are delicate and can toughen if overcooked.

| FOOD | Container | Cover | Power Level & Time | | Comments |
|---|---|---|---|---|---|
| **EGGS**<br>Scrambled | Glass measuring cup or casserole | No | Med-High | ¾ to 1 min. per egg. | Place 1 teaspoon butter per egg in dish. Microwave at High until melted. Scramble the eggs with the butter and 1 tablespoon milk per egg. Place in oven and microwave for ½ of total time. Stir set portions from the outside to the center. Finish cooking. Allow to stand 1 or 2 minutes. |
| Basic eggs | Buttered custard cup | Plastic wrap | Medium | ¾ to 1 min. per egg | Puncture membrane of yolk to prevent bursting. Rearrange, if necessary. |
| Poached eggs (4 maximum) | 1½-qt. casserole | Casserole lid | High<br><br>High | 6 to 8 min. Boil 2 cups water<br><br>½ to ¾ min. per egg | Heat 2 cups hot tap water 6 to 8 minutes on High. Break eggs onto plate, puncture membrane. Slip eggs gently into water. Cover. Cook according to chart. Remove with slotted spoon. |
| Fluffy Omelet (3 eggs) | 9" pie plate | No | High<br><br>Medium | Melt butter 1 min.<br>6 to 8 min. | Cook until set. Sprinkle cheese over omelet. Microwave ½ to 1 minute until cheese is slightly melted. |
| Quiche | Microwave safe 1-qt. measure and 9-in. quiche dish | No | Med-High<br><br>Med-High | Filling: 2 to 3 min.<br>Quiche: 5 to 7 min. | Combine and microwave filling, stirring every 2 minutes. Pour filling into precooked shell. Microwave additional time shown at left. |
| **CHEESE**<br>Fondue | Microwave safe 2-qt. dish | Cover or plastic wrap | High<br><br>Medium | To heat wine 5 min.<br><br>5 min. | Use 1 cup wine and 3 tablespoons flour per lb. of shredded cheese. Add cheese, flour and seasonings to hot wine and microwave at Medium, stirring every minute, until smooth. |

# Breads

1. Crust on breads will be soft. Outside color of foods will be same as color of batter (outsides will not brown). If desired, sprinkle top of batter with cinnamon-sugar mixture, chopped nuts or other topping for brown color. Or, increase brown color on upside down breads by lining dish before microwaving with brown sugar caramel mixture.

| FOOD | Container | Cover | Power Level & Time | | Comments |
|---|---|---|---|---|---|
| Coffee Cakes From refrigerated biscuits | 8-in. tube dish* | No | Medium | 6 to 7 min. | Arrange biscuits over brown sugar-butter topping before microwaving. Invert to serve. |
| Corn Bread | 8 to 9-in. tube dish* | No | Med-High | 8 to 9 min. | For flavorful browned topping sprinkle cooking dish with finely chopped canned French fried onions before microwaving. Turn out of pan upside down to serve. |
| Muffins | Paper-lined muffin cups (Do not use foil liners) | No | Med-High<br>1 Muffin:<br>2 to 4:<br>3 to 6: | <br>¾ to 1¼ min.<br>1 to 3 min.<br>3 to 4½ min. | Use microwave muffin container or homemade muffin cups (made by cutting down paper hot drink cups). |
| Quick Breads, Loaf | Glass loaf dish | No | Med-High | 12 to 14 min. | When done, toothpick inserted in center will come out clean. Let stand 15 min. before turning out of dish. Cool. |

*If tube dish is unavailable, use microwave safe 8" round dish with drinking glass placed open-side-up in center.

# 12 Vegetables

1. Always use microwave-safe utensils, glass or plastic. Cook most vegetables with tight cover to steam them. Exceptions are potatoes cooked in their skins and watery vegetables which need no water added for steam.
2. Do not salt tops of vegetables before microwaving. If desired, add salt to water in dish before adding vegetables. Salt can sometimes cause brown spots on vegetables during microwaving.
3. Cooking time for vegetables affects finished taste and texture. Minimum time on chart gives fresh taste and crisp-tender texture. For soft texture with well-developed flavor, cook maximum time or longer.
4. Size of pieces affect cooking time. Large pieces generally take longer than small uniform pieces.
5. Just as when cooking conventionally, vegetable mixtures should have similar densities or degrees of firmness in order to cook together successfully. Firm, crisp vegetables like carrots, cauliflower and broccoli microwave together well. If microwaving a firm vegetable with a soft one (carrots and peas, for example) cut the carrots in julienne strips so they will cook as fast as the peas. Or, start cooking larger carrot pieces first, and add peas during last few minutes.

| VEGETABLES | Container | Cover | Power Level & Time | | Comments |
|---|---|---|---|---|---|
| Slices, pieces | Casserole | Yes | 1 lb.: High<br>2 lb.: High | 8 to 17 min.<br>15 to 20 min. | Add ¼ to ½ cup water. If frozen reduce time 3 to 5 minutes because vegetables are blanched. |
| Whole, halves or large or starchy vegetables (potatoes, winter squash, cauliflower, etc.) | Potatoes: Cook on oven shelf (no container) Other vegetables: Square dish or casserole | Potatoes: No<br><br>Winter squash, cauliflower, etc.: Yes | 1 lb. (3 to 4): High<br><br>2 lb. (6 to 8): High | 12 to 20 min.<br><br>16 to 20 min. | Prick skin of potatoes before cooking. |
| Watery (tomatoes, summer squash) | Casserole | Yes | 1 lb. (3 to 4): High<br><br>2 lb. (6 to 8): High | 7 to 12 min.<br><br>10 to 16 min. | Cut in pieces or halves. No additional water needed. |
| Vegetable casseroles | Casserole | Yes | Casserole made with raw vegetables: High<br><br>Precooked vegetables: High | 18 to 20 min.<br><br>12 to 14 min. | Use large enough casserole to allow for boiling in dish. |
| Stir-fry vegetables | 2-qt. casserole | Yes | High | 12 to 14 min. (6 to 8 servings) | To stir fry one type of vegetable, substitute 1 tablespoon oil for water and follow techniques on page 40. |
| Blanching fresh vegetables for freezing | Glass casserole | Yes | High | 3 to 7 min. | Blanch only 1-lb. or 1-qt. prepared vegetables at a time. Place in 1 to 2-qt. casserole with ¼ to ½ cup water. Blanched vegetables will have bright even color and will be slightly softened. Cool drained blanched vegetables immediately by plunging in container of ice water. |
| Frozen Vegetables | | | | | See page 40. |

# Gravies and Sauces

1. No cover is needed, except for thick chunky spaghetti sauce.
2. Microwaved sauces do not need to be stirred constantly but most should be whisked vigorously with wire whisk once or twice while microwaving.
3. Vary basic white sauce by adding cheese, egg yolks, cream or dry milk solids. Add flour with mayonnaise or wine.

| FOOD | Container | Cover | Power Level & Time | | Comments |
|---|---|---|---|---|---|
| Gravies and sauces thickened with flour or cornstarch | Glass measure or bowl | No | 1 cup: High | 4 to 5½ min. | Microwave fat, flour and salt together to melt and blend. Whisk in liquid and finish cooking. Increase time 1 to 2 minutes per additional cup of sauce. |
| Thin, liquid sauces (Au jus, clam, etc.) | Casserole | No | 1 cup: High | 4 to 5 min. | Add cornstarch-water mixture to heated ingredients. Stir well and microwave to finish. |
| Melted butter sauces,<br><br>Clarified butter | Glass measure | No | ½ cup: High<br><br>½ cup: High | 1½ to 2 min.<br><br>2½ to 3 min. | Microwave butter just to melt. For clarified butter, bring to boil then let stand until layers separate. Pour off and use clear top layer. |
| Thick spaghetti, barbecue or sweet/sour sauces | Casserole, large bowl | Yes (spaghetti) | 2 cups: High | 4 to 7 min. | Stir ingredients together then microwave, stirring after half of time. Let stand 5 to 10 minutes to develop flavor. |

# Pasta and Rice

1. Always use microwave-safe utensil, glass or plastic.
2. Use hottest tap water as directed below; there is less evaporation in a microwave oven. Add 1 to 2 teaspoons salt and 1 teaspoon oil.
3. For rice or Minute rice use the same or slightly greater amount of water as with conventional boiling. Add regular amount salt.
4. Cover pasta and rice tightly while microwaving. When using plastic wrap, turn back one corner to vent.
5. Stir or rearrange after half of cooking time. Drain pasta immediately after microwaving.
6. Microwave times are about the same as conventional cook times.

| PASTA and RICE | Container | Cover | Power Level & Time | | Comments |
|---|---|---|---|---|---|
| Macaroni (7 to 8-oz.) | 3-qt. straight sided bowl | Plastic wrap | High | 12 min. | Add 3 cups water. Stir after 8 minutes. For rotini type, check for doneness after 10 minutes. |
| Spaghetti (8-oz.) | 3-qt. straight sided bowl | Plastic wrap | High | 13 to 14 min. | Break in half. Add 6 cups water. Stir after 8 minutes. |
| Egg noodles (8-oz.) | 3-qt. straight sided bowl | Plastic wrap | High | 6 to 10 min. | Add 5 cups water. Stir after 5 minutes. Time is the same for spinach or regular noodles. |
| Rice, regular long grain (1 cup) | 2-qt. casserole | Plastic wrap | High | 16 min. | Add 2¼ cups water. Stir after 10 minutes. Let stand, covered, 5 minutes before serving. |
| Rice, packaged precooked(Minute) (1½ cups) | 2-qt. casserole | Lid or plastic wrap | High | 6 min. | Add 1½ cups water and rice. Stir after 2 minutes. |

# Cereal

1. Always use microwave-safe utensils, glass or plastic. Use large enough container to avoid boilover.
2. Start with hottest tap water to shorten cooking time.
3. Do not cover (prevents boilover).
4. Stir halfway through cooking time.

| FOOD | Container | Cover | Power Level & Time | | Comments |
|---|---|---|---|---|---|
| Oatmeal, quick | China or pottery bowl, paper bowl | No | High | 2½ to 3 min. per serving | Mix cereal, salt and hottest tap water before microwaving. Stir before serving. |

NOTE: To microwave single-serving packet of instant oatmeal, follow package directions for amount of hot tap water and microwave at High for 2 to 2½ minutes.

| | | | | | |
|---|---|---|---|---|---|
| Oatmeal, old fashioned | 1-qt. casserole or bowl for 1 serving | No | High | 4 to 5 min. for 1 serving | Mix cereal with hottest tap water. Use 2-qt. casserole for more than one serving. Increase time about 2 minutes for each additional serving. |
| Grits, quick | China or pottery bowl, paper bowl | No | High | 4 to 5 min. for 1 serving | Mix cereal with hottest tap water. Increase casserole size and microwave time by 2 to 3 minutes per additional serving. |

NOTE: To microwave single-serving packet of instant grits, follow directions for amount of water and microwave at High for ½ to 1 minute.

| | | | | | |
|---|---|---|---|---|---|
| Cream of wheat, regular | 1-qt. casserole or bowl | No | High | 4 to 5 min. for 1 serving | Mix cereal with hottest tap water. Use 2-qt. casserole for more than 1 serving. Increase time 1 to 2 minutes per additional serving. |
| Cream of wheat, quick | China or pottery bowl, paper bowl | No | High | 2½ to 3 min. per serving | Mix cereal with hottest tap water. Use 2-qt. casserole for more than 1 serving and increase time 1 to 2 minutes per serving. |
| Cream of rice | China or pottery bowl, paper bowl | No | High | 1½ to 2 min. for 1 serving | Mix cereal with hottest tap water. Use 2-qt. casserole for more than 1 serving. Increase time about 1 minute per additional serving. |

# 14 Cakes and Desserts

1. Always use microwave-safe utensils, either glass or plastic.
2. Before adding measured amount of batter, grease dishes, but do not flour. Or, for easy removal, line dish with wax paper.
3. Rotate dishes 1/4 turn every 5 minutes unless directed otherwise.
4. Cakes are done when toothpick or long skewer stuck in center comes out clean.
5. Cool cake in dish set directly on heat-proof surface or wooden board 10 to 45 minutes (check package directions for some large special cakes) before inverting to finish cooling.
6. Crust on cakes will be soft. Refrigerate cake if firm exterior is desirable for frosting.
7. Fruit desserts will be fresh looking and tasting.

| FOOD | Container | Cover | Power Level & Time | | Comments |
|---|---|---|---|---|---|
| **CAKES** | | | | | |
| Commercial mix | 8-in. round or square | No | Low, then High | 5 min. 4½ to 5½ min. | Use 2 cups batter. Rotate ¼ turn every 3 minutes. Let stand 10 minutes before inverting to cool. |
| | 14 to 16-cup fluted tube cake pan | | Low, then High | 10 min. 9 to 10 min. | Use all batter. Rotate ¼ turn every 5 minutes. Let stand 15 to 45 minutes before inverting to cool. |
| Basic butter cake | Greased 8-in. round dish | No | High | 8 to 9 min. | Rotate ½ turn after 4 minutes. Let stand on heat-proof counter or wooden board to cool 15 minutes. |
| Pineapple upside down cake | 8-in. round dish | Wax paper | Med-High | 12 to 13 min. | When done, toothpick stuck in cakes comes out clean. Invert cake onto plate, let dish stand over cake a few minutes. |
| Cupcakes—6 | Paper lined cupcaker | Wax paper | Med-High | 3 to 4½ min. | When cooking several cupcakes, you may notice some will be done before others. If so, remove cupcakes as they are done and continue cooking the rest a few seconds more. |
| Bar cookies | 8-in. square dish | No | Med-High | 10 to 12 min. | Grease dish before adding batter. Rotate dish ½ turn after half of time. Cut when cool. |
| Baked apples or pears | Microwave safe dish or casserole | Lid or plastic wrap | High | 2½ to 4 min. per piece | Pierce fruit or peel to prevent bursting. |

# Candies

1. Always use microwave-safe utensils, glass or plastic. For easy cleanup, melt chocolate in paper wrappers seam side up, or place chocolate in paper bowl to melt.
2. Candies which are boiled become very hot, be sure to handle cooking containers carefully.

| FOOD | Container | Cover | Power Level & Time | | Comments |
|---|---|---|---|---|---|
| S'Mores | Paper napkin or paper plate | No | Med-High | 30 seconds | Cover graham cracker with chocolate and marshmallow. Microwave. |
| Caramel apples | 1 pint (2-cup) measure | No | High | 2 to 3 min. | Unwrap half of a 14-oz. package of caramels into measuring cup. Add 1 tablespoon water. Microwave and stir smooth before dipping 4 apples into mixture. |
| Marshmallow crisp | 8-in. square dish | Yes | High | 1 min. to melt butter 4 min. to melt marshmallows | In 8-in. square dish melt ¼ cup butter. Add 10-oz. package marshmallows. Cover with wax paper and microwave to melt. Stir in 4 cups crispy rice cereal. |
| Chocolate bark | 1½-qt. casserole or bowl | Yes | High | 4 to 5 min. | Place 12-oz. semi-sweet chocolate pieces in container. Microwave to melt. Add 1 cup whole toasted almonds. Spread over wax paper on cookie sheet. Chill until firm. |

# Microwave Utensil Guide

| TYPE OF UTENSIL | MICROWAVE USES |
|---|---|
| **Foil-lined Paper Bags, Boxes and Baking Trays**<br>**Metal or part metal pots, Pans, Thermometers, Skewers and Foil Trays** | Avoid. Use only foil trays ¾-in. deep or less. Foil or metal will reflect microwaves, thus preventing even heating. Arcing can occur if foil is closer than 1-in. to oven walls. |
| **Boilable Hard and Soft Plastics, such as:**<br>Rubbermaid | Cooking ground beef (colander). Defrosting. Heating. |
| **Glass jars, such as:** for baby foods, vegetables, entrees, syrups, salad dressing. | **Avoid heating baby food in jars,** especially meat and egg mixtures.<br>Remove metal caps to warm syrup or soften salad dressing from refrigerator. |
| **Handmade Pottery, Porcelain, Stoneware** | Cooking and heating. |
| **Microwave Plastics such as:**<br>Anchor Hocking Microwave, Bangor Plastic, Mister Microwave, Nordic Ware, Republic, Rubbermaid, Tara, Wearever Nupac. | Cooking. |
| **Paper or Styrofoam Plates and Cups** | Heating and serving foods and beverages. Styrofoam should be used for short-term heating to low temperatures and for serving. |
| **Oven Glass such as:**<br>Anchor Hocking, Fire King, Glassbake, Heller, Jena, Pyrex | Cooking and heating. |
| **Regular Dinnerware, such as:**<br>Corelle by Corning, Dansk Generation, Denby, El Camino, Franciscan, International Stoneware, Lenox Temperware, Marsh, Mikasa, Pfalzgraff | Heating and some cooking. |
| **Unsuitable Dinnerware, such as:**<br>Corning Centura, Fitz and Floyd Oven-to-table Ware, Malamine, Dishes with metal trim. | None. |
| **Paper Towels and Napkins, Wax Paper** | Cooking bacon. Absorbing moisture and preventing spatters. Heating and serving sandwiches or appetizers. Light covering to hold in steam. |
| **Glass-Ceramic (Pyroceram), such as:**<br>Corning Ware, Progression G. by Noritake | Cooking and heating. |
| **Plastic Wrap, Cooking Bags, Boil-in-bags, Storage Bags** | Covering to hold in steam (wrap). Cooking (cooking and boil-in-bags). Heating (storage bags). |
| **Specialty Glass-Ceramic and Porcelain, such as:**<br>El Camino, F.B. Rogers, Heller, Marsh Industries, Pfaltzgraff, Shafford | Recommended for microwave oven-to-table cooking of special foods. |

## How to Convert Conventional Recipes for Microwaving

Before converting your recipe, study it in terms of microwaving. Is it one of the many foods which microwave well? Look for cooking techniques which are similar to microwaving techniques, such as covering, steaming or cooking in sauce or liquid. If the food requires a crisp, fried crust or very dry surface, you will prefer to cook it conventionally. Some recipes may not be exactly the same when microwaved, but you will be pleased with the results.

If the food is suitable for microwaving, refer to a simlar recipe for cooking techniques, power level, timing and possible changes in ingredients.

Many recipes will not need changing. Moist, rich cakes, candies and moist meat loaves are examples.

Since liquids do not evaporate as much when microwaved, reduce the amount or add more thickening to sauces and gravies. Reduce some seasonings: lack of evaporation intensities flavors. Salt meats and vegetables after cooking. If an ingredient takes longer to microwave than others, substitute one which is precooked or quick-cooking, as we have done in the following example.

### Conventional Spanish Rice

COOKING TIME: 45 to 50 min., total

*Use Chuck,* — **1 lb. ground beef** .... In 10-in. skillet crumble ground beef. Cook over medium high heat 10 minutes, uncovered. — *Use 2 qt. casserole* — *Skip*

*Omit.* — **1½ cups water** ........
*Substitute 1 cup precooked rice* — **¾ cup long grain rice**
**2 tablespoons chili powder**
*Reduce* — **2 tablespoons instant minced onion**
**2 teaspoons salt**
**⅛ teaspoon pepper**
**1 can (1-lb, 12-oz.) tomatoes**

Add water, rice, chili powder, onion, salt, pepper and tomatoes. Stir very well. Cover and cook over medium heat 35 to 40 minutes.

*Microwave at High 12 to 14 minutes, stirring after 6 minutes.*

Makes 4 to 6 servings

### Microwave Spanish Rice

POWER LEVEL: High
MICROWAVE TIME: 12 to 14 min., total

**1 lb. ground chuck beef** ..
**1 cup packaged precooked rice (Minute)**
**1 can (1-lb. 12-oz.) tomatoes**
**1 tablespoon instant minced onion**
**2 tablespoons chili powder**
**2 teaspoons salt**
**⅛ teaspoon pepper**

Into 2-qt. casserole crumble beef. Add remaining ingredients and mix well, cutting tomatoes to distribute evenly. Cover. **Microwave at High 12 to 14 Minutes,** stirring after 6 minutes. If top of food appears dry during cooking, stir again, then return to oven to finish cooking.

Makes 4 to 6 servings

## Cooking Techniques for Microwaving

**Covering.** In both conventional and microwave cooking, covers hold in moisture and speed heating. Conventionally, partial covering allows excess steam to escape. Venting plastic wrap or covering with wax paper serves the same purpose when microwaving.

**Arranging Food on Oven Shelf.** In conventional baking, you position foods, such as cake layers or potatoes, so that hot air can flow around them. When microwaving, you arrange foods in a ring, so that all sides are exposed to microwave energy.

**Stirring.** In range-top cooking, you stir foods up from the bottom to help them heat evenly. When microwaving you stir cooked portions from the outside to the center. Foods which require constant stirring conventionally will need only occasional stirring.

**Turning over.** In range top cooking you turn over foods such as hamburgers, so both sides can directly contact hot pan. When microwaving, turning is often needed during defrosting, or when cooking foods such as hamburgers from the frozen state.

**Standing Time.** In conventional cooking, foods such as roasts or cakes are allowed to stand to finish cooking or set. Standing time is especially important in microwave cooking. Note that the microwaved cake is not placed on a cooling rack.

**Shielding.** In a conventional oven you shield chicken breasts or baked foods to prevent over-browning. When defrosting, you use small strips of foil to shield thin parts, such as the tips of wings and legs on poultry, which would cook before larger parts were defrosted.

**Prick Foods to Release Pressure.** Steam builds up pressure in foods which are tightly covered by a skin or membrane. Prick potatoes (as you do conventionally), egg yolks and chicken livers to prevent bursting.

**Rotating.** Occasionally, repositioning a dish in the oven helps food cook evenly. To rotate ½ turn, turn the dish until the side which was to the back of the oven is to the front. To rotate ¼ turn, turn the dish until the side which was to the back of the oven is to the side.

## Effects of Food Characteristics on Microwaving

**Density of Food.** In both conventional and microwave cooking, dense foods, such as a potato, take longer to cook or heat than light, porous foods, such as a piece of cake, bread or a roll.

**Round Shapes.** Since microwaves penetrate foods to about 1-in. from top, bottom and sides, round shapes and rings cook more evenly. Corners receive more energy and may overcook. This may also happen when cooking conventionally.

**Delicacy.** Foods with a delicate texture are best cooked at lower power settings to avoid toughening.

**Natural Moisture** of food affects how it cooks. Very moist foods cook evenly because microwave energy is attracted to water molecules. Food uneven in moisture should be covered or allowed to stand so heat can disperse evenly.

**Piece Size.** Small pieces cook faster than large ones. Pieces which are similar in size and shape cook more evenly. With large pieces of food, reduce the power setting for even cooking.

**Shape of Food.** In both types of cooking, thin areas cook faster than thick ones. This can be controlled in microwaving by placing thick pieces near the outside edge, and thin pieces in the center.

**Starting Temperature.** Foods taken from the freezer or refrigerator take longer to cook than foods at room temperature. Timings in our recipes are based on the temperatures at which you normally store the foods.

**Quantity of Food.** In both types of cooking, small amounts usually take less time than large ones. This is most apparent in microwave cooking, where time is directly related to the number of servings.

## Croutons Italiano

POWER LEVEL: High
MICROWAVE TIME: 7 to 9 min., total

| | |
|---|---|
| **3 cups bread cubes** . . . . . . . . | In 8-in. square dish place cubes. **Microwave at High 4 to 5 Minutes,** stirring every 2 minutes, until cubes begin to dry. |
| **1 tablespoon Italian herb seasoning** . . . . . . <br> **¼ teaspoon garlic salt** <br> **¼ cup melted butter** | Sprinkle herb seasoning and garlic salt evenly over bread cubes. Drizzle with butter, tossing to coat cubes. |

**Microwave at High 3 to 4 Minutes,** stirring every minute, until crisp and dry.

Makes 6 cups

## Toasted Butter Pecans

POWER LEVEL: High
MICROWAVE TIME: 7 to 8 min., total

| | |
|---|---|
| **1 lb. pecan halves (about 4 cups)** . . <br> **1 tablespoon seasoned salt** <br> **¼ cup butter** | In 1½-qt. casserole place pecan halves. Sprinkle with seasoned salt. Cut butter into 4 pieces and arrange evenly over top. |

**Microwave at High 7 to 8 Minutes.** Mix to evenly distribute butter. Serve warm or cold.

Makes 1 pound

## Soft Smokey Cheese Ball

POWER LEVEL: High
MICROWAVE TIME: 2 to 2¼ min., total

| | |
|---|---|
| **1 roll-shaped pkg.** . . <br> **(6-oz.) smokey cheese spread** <br> **2 pkgs. (3-oz. each) cream cheese** <br> **1 teaspoon Worcestershire sauce** <br> **1 cup (4-oz.) shredded sharp cheddar cheese** | Unwrap cheeses. In 1½-qt. casserole place smokey cheese. **Microwave at High 1 Minute.** Add cream cheese. **Microwave at High 1 to 1¼ Minutes** more, until cheeses can be mixed together. Add Worcestershire sauce and blend mixture well. Stir in shredded cheese. Mixture should remain gold-flecked. |
| **½ cup chopped parsley** . . . . . . <br> **½ cup chopped pecans** | Chill cheese mixture about 15 to 30 minutes in freezer or about 1 hour in refrigerator, until it can be formed into a ball with the hands. Roll cheese ball in parsley, then pecans. Chill to set. Serve with crackers. |

Makes 1 cheese ball, about 1-lb.

## Nachos

POWER LEVEL: High
MICROWAVE TIME: ¾ to 1 min., per plate

| | |
|---|---|
| **Large corn chips** . . <br> **(plain or taco flavored)** <br> **Jalapeno bean dip or refried beans** <br> **Hot pepper cheese** | Mound about 1 teaspoon bean dip or refried bean mixture on each tortilla corn chip. Top with ⅛-in. thick slice of cheese, to cover bean dip. Place 8 to 12 pieces in circle on paper plate or small pottery plate, leaving center space open. **Microwave at High ¾ to 1 Minute,** until cheese is melted. |

## Appetizer Franks

*If desired, 2 cans (4-oz. each) Vienna sausages, drained and halved, may be substituted for frankfurters.*

POWER LEVEL: Medium High
MICROWAVE TIME: 2 to 3 min., per plate

| | |
|---|---|
| **3 frankfurters** . . . . . . <br> **¼ cup apricot preserves or apple jelly** <br> **1 tablespoon prepared mustard** | Cut frankfurters into eighths and arrange in circle on plastic coated paper plate. Mix together preserves and mustard and spread over pieces. Stick each piece with wooden pick. **Microwave at Medium High 2 to 3 Minutes,** until hot. |

**Chili Franks:** Substitute chili sauce for preserves and mustard.

Makes 24 hors d'oeuvres

## Chili Con Queso Dip

*Served fondue style, and accompanied by a salad, Chili Con Queso makes a nice informal luncheon. Dip is very thick and should be served with sturdy dippers such as large tortilla chips.*

POWER LEVEL: Medium High        TEMP: 140°
MICROWAVE TIME: 8 to 9 min., total

| | |
|---|---|
| **1 lb. block** . . . . . . . <br> **pasteurized processed cheese, cubed** <br> **1 can (1-lb.) chili with beans** | In 1½-qt. casserole stir together diced cheese and chili. |

Insert temperature probe so tip is in center of dip. Attach cable end at receptacle. **Microwave at Medium High. Set Temp, Set 140°.** Stir once.

When oven signals, stir well. Let stand a few minutes before serving. Serve with tortilla chips.

Makes about 3 cups

## Bacon-Wrapped Chicken Livers

*This is often known by its Polynesian name of Rumaki. For convenience, you can prepare ahead of time and store in the refrigerator until time to microwave. Because the chicken livers cook more quickly than the bacon, it is important to precook the bacon before using it to wrap the livers.*

POWER LEVEL: High and Medium High
MICROWAVE TIME: 7 to 9 min., per plate

| | |
|---|---|
| **1 lb. thinly sliced .... bacon** | **Microwave at High 1 Minute,** in the package, until slices easily separate. Divide bacon slices between 4 paper towel lined paper plates. Cover with paper towel. Microwave one plate at a time. **Microwave at Medium High 4 Minutes.** |
| **½ can (8-oz.) water .. chestnuts** | Drain and cut each water chestnut in half. |
| **½ lb. chicken ........ livers (about 10)** | Rinse and drain livers. Cut in half. |

Sprinkle bacon strips lightly with ground cloves and brown sugar. Place one piece of chicken liver and one piece of water chestnut at the end of each bacon strip. Roll up, securing with a toothpick. Arrange 10 in a circle on a paper towel lined paper plate. Cover with paper towel. **Microwave at High 2 to 4 Minutes,** rotating dish ¼ turn after 1½ minutes. When microwaving from refrigerator temperature, increase time for each plate ½ to 1 minute.

Makes 20 hors d'oeuvres

## Curried Beef Balls

POWER LEVEL: High
MICROWAVE TIME: 8 to 10 min., total

| | |
|---|---|
| **½ cup butter ...... flavored cracker crumbs or slightly crushed herb seasoned stuffing mix** <br> **⅓ cup evaporated milk** <br> **¼ teaspoon salt** <br> **1½ to 2 teaspoons curry powder** <br> **1 lb. ground chuck beef** | In large mixing bowl thoroughly combine crumbs, milk, salt and curry powder. Add beef and blend well. Shape meat mixture into 48 (1-in.) balls. |

In 8-in. square dish place about 24 balls. Cover with wax paper. **Microwave at High 4 to 5 Minutes.** Repeat with other half of beef balls.

Makes 4 dozen hors d'oeuvres

*Tacos*

## Tacos

POWER LEVEL: High
MICROWAVE TIME: 14 to 16 min., total

| | |
|---|---|
| **1 lb. ground chuck .. beef** <br> **½ cup chopped onion** <br> **½ cup chopped green pepper** <br> **1 clove garlic, minced** | In 2-qt. casserole break up ground beef in very small chunks. Add onion, green pepper and garlic. Cover. **Microwave at High 8 Minutes,** stirring after 3 minutes. Drain well. |
| **1 can (8-oz.) ....... tomato sauce** <br> **1 teaspoon Worcestershire sauce** <br> **⅛ to ¼ teaspoon cayenne pepper** <br> **½ teaspoon chili powder** <br> **½ teaspoon salt** | Add tomato sauce, Worcestershire sauce, pepper, chili powder and salt. Cover. **Microwave at High 6 to 8 Minutes,** stirring after 3 minutes. |

Use meat to fill prebaked, packaged taco shells, filling about half full. Finish tacos by topping with 2 or more of the following: shredded lettuce, shredded cheese, chopped tomatoes and chopped onions. Add hot sauce if desired.

Makes 12 tacos

## Bacon Poles

POWER LEVEL: High
MICROWAVE TIME: 3 to 3½ min., total

| | |
|---|---|
| **3 strips bacon ......** <br> **6 long, thin garlic bread sticks or sesame bread sticks** | With scissors, cut bacon strips in half lengthwise, making 2 long, thin strips from each slice. Wrap one strip in a spiral "barber pole fashion" around each bread stick. |

Place 2 paper towels on paper plate or microwave safe dinner plate. Distribute wrapped bread sticks so they don't touch each other. Cover with paper towel. **Microwave at High 3 to 3½ Minutes,** rotating plate ½ turn after 2 minutes, until bacon is cooked.

Makes 6 appetizers

# 20 Ground Beef

## Hamburger Patty Stew

*When arranging this casserole, be sure that the top layer of beef patties is well covered with vegetables or it will overcook.*

POWER LEVEL: High
MICROWAVE TIME: 30 to 35 min., total

| | |
|---|---|
| 2 medium .......... potatoes<br>2 medium carrots<br>2 medium onions | Peel vegetables and thinly slice. |
| 1 lb. ground chuck .. beef<br>1 teaspoon salt<br>⅛ teaspoon pepper<br>¼ cup water<br>Paprika | Form beef into 12 small flat patties. In 2-qt. casserole layer half of beef patties then half of vegetables, sprinkling layers with salt and pepper. Repeat. Add water. Press down into casserole. Sprinkle with paprika. Cover. **Microwave at High 30 to 35 Minutes.** Let stand 5 minutes before serving. |

Makes 4 servings

## Sloppy Joes

POWER LEVEL: High
MICROWAVE TIME: 14 to 17 min., total

| | |
|---|---|
| 1½ lbs. ground .... chuck beef<br>⅔ cup finely chopped onion<br>½ cup diced celery<br>¼ cup diced green pepper | In 2-qt. casserole crumble beef. Add onion, celery and green pepper. Cover. **Microwave at High 8 to 10 Minutes,** stirring every 3 minutes. Drain meat well. |
| ½ cup ketchup ......<br>1 tablespoon Worcestershire sauce<br>½ teaspoon salt<br>⅛ teaspoon pepper | To cooked meat mixture, add ketchup, Worcestershire sauce, salt and pepper. Cover. **Microwave at High 6 to 7 Minutes,** until hot. To serve, stir, then spoon onto buns or crusty French rolls. |

Makes 6 to 8 sandwiches

**Sloppy Joes with Cheese:** Add 1 cup (4-oz.) shredded cheddar cheese to meat mixture along with ketchup.

**Sloppy Joes with Beans:** Add 1 can (16-oz.) pork and beans to meat mixture along with ketchup.

## Layered Taco Salad

POWER LEVEL: High
MICROWAVE TIME: 21 to 24 min., total

| | |
|---|---|
| 1 pounds ground .... chuck beef<br>½ cup chopped onion (1 small)<br>1 cup chopped green pepper (about 1)<br>1 can (16-oz.) hot chili beans in chili gravy (not drained) | In 2-qt. casserole crumble beef. Add onion and green pepper. Cover. **Microwave at High for 10 Minutes,** stirring every 3 minutes. Drain well. Add chili beans. Recover and **Microwave at High for 5 to 6 Minutes,** until hot. Keep warm. |
| 1 can (10-oz.) mild .. enchilada sauce<br>1 can (8-oz.) tomato sauce<br>1 can (8-oz.) mild taco sauce | In 1½-qt. casserole combine sauces. **Microwave at High for 6 to 8 Minutes,** stirring after 5 minutes. |
| 6 to 10 ounce ...... package corn chips or tortilla chips<br>1 cup (4-oz.) shredded cheddar or mozzarella cheese<br>4 cups shredded lettuce (about ½ head)<br>2 cups chopped tomatoes | Into 4-qt. salad bowl or casserole layer corn chips, meat mixture, one half of cheese, lettuce and tomatoes. Pour sauce over entire casserole and sprinkle with remaining cheese. Serve immediately. Toss just before serving if desired. |

Makes 6 servings

## Chili

POWER LEVEL: High
MICROWAVE TIME: 30 min., total

| | |
|---|---|
| 1 lb. ground chuck .. beef<br>1 can (14½ to 16-oz.) tomatoes, undrained<br>1 can (19-oz.) kidney beans, undrained<br>½ cup finely chopped green pepper<br>2 teaspoons instant minced onion<br>1 to 2 tablespoons chili powder<br>1½ teaspoons salt | Into 2-qt. casserole crumble beef. Mix in tomatoes, beans, green pepper, onion, chili powder and salt. Cover and **Microwave at High for 30 Minutes,** stirring after 15 minutes. When oven signals, stir and let chili stand about 10 minutes to blend flavors before serving. |

Makes 4 to 6 servings

Meatballs microwave exceptionally well and turn brown after a short standing time, so they need no special browning. These recipes are good examples of favorite ways to cook meatballs. However, it is not at all difficult to adapt your own favorite recipes: just be sure to plan for the standing time.

## Basic Meatballs

POWER LEVEL: High
MICROWAVE TIME: 9 to 10 min., total

| | |
|---|---|
| 1 **lb. ground chuck beef**<br>1 **egg**<br>½ **cup fine bread crumbs**<br>3 **tablespoons milk, tomato sauce or water**<br>1 **teaspoon salt**<br>¼ **teaspoon paprika**<br>⅛ **teaspoon pepper** | Mix together beef, egg, crumbs, milk, salt, paprika and pepper. Shape into 12 balls and arrange in a circle in 9 or 10-in. pie plate. Cover with wax paper. **Microwave at High 9 to 10 Minutes** until done. Rotate dish ½ turn after half the time. If desired, serve with Classic Italian Sauce, page 34.<br><br>Makes 12 meatballs |

VARIATIONS:
Add one of the following flavor combinations:
1 tablespoon Worcestershire sauce and ¼ cup chopped onion
1 tablespoon steak sauce and 1 clove crushed garlic (or ½ teaspoon garlic powder)
1 tablespoon chili sauce and ¼ cup finely chopped green pepper
2 tablespoons red wine and 1 teaspoon oregano

## Swedish Meatballs

POWER LEVEL: High
MICROWAVE TIME: 24 to 28 min., total

| | |
|---|---|
| 2 **lbs. ground chuck beef**<br>2 **cups soft bread crumbs**<br>½ **cup milk**<br>1 **egg**<br>1 **pkg. (½ of 2¾-oz. box) onion soup mix**<br>½ **teaspoon salt**<br>½ **teaspoon nutmeg** | Mix together beef, crumbs, milk, egg, soup mix, salt and nutmeg. Shape meat mixture into 36 balls. Cook 12 at a time in 9-in. pie plate. Cover with wax paper. **Microwave at High 6 to 7 Minutes.** Remove meatballs from pie plate to 3-quart straight-sided casserole and keep warm, reserving meat drippings in 4 cup measure. Repeat twice. |
| 2 **tablespoons unsifted all-purpose flour**<br>1 **cup milk**<br>2 **teaspoons browning sauce**<br>1 **cup dairy sour cream (8-oz.)** | To ¼ cup drippings in measure, add flour, stirring until smooth. Gradually stir in milk and browning sauce. **Microwave at High 3 to 4 Minutes,** stirring every minute, until boiling. Add sour cream. Stir well. Pour over meatballs in casserole. **Microwave at High 3 Minutes,** until hot. Serve over noodles or rice. |

Makes 36 meatballs (1½-in.)

**Arrange** meatballs in a ring around the edge of a 9 or 10-in. pie plate. For small meatballs, form a double row.

## Meatballs in Onion Broth

POWER LEVEL: High
MICROWAVE TIME: 20 to 27 min., total

| | |
|---|---|
| 2 **pounds very lean ground veal, pork and beef mixture**<br>1 **medium onion, finely chopped**<br>2 **eggs**<br>2 **tablespoons flour**<br>2 **tablespoons dry onion soup mix**<br>1 **teaspoon salt**<br>¼ **teaspoon pepper** | In medium bowl mix together ground meat, onion, eggs, flour, soup mix, salt and pepper. Form into 16 medium-sized balls (up to ¼ cup per ball). Arrange meatballs in 8×8×2-in. dish. |
| **Boiling water**<br>2 **bay leaves**<br>2 **tablespoons dry onion soup mix**<br>1 **teaspoon salt**<br>1 **teaspoon browning sauce (optional)** | Add 2 cups boiling water, bay leaves, soup mix, salt and browning sauce to meatballs. Cover dish with plastic wrap. **Microwave at High 20 Minutes,** rotating dish after ½ of time. Thicken broth if desired. |

**To Thicken Broth:** Remove meatballs from broth and keep warm. Skim fat from broth in dish. Into hot broth in dish, stir mixture of 2 tablespoons flour and 3 tablespoons water. Add additional dry onion soup mix for onion gravy. **Microwave at High 6 to 7 Minutes,** stirring every 2 minutes.

Makes 16 meatballs

Round flat meat loaves cook fastest at High power. Loaf shaped meat loaves need Medium High power to evenly cook the center without overcooking the edges.

## Cheese Stuffed Meat Loaf

*This meat loaf tastes like a cheeseburger and will be popular with your family.*

POWER LEVEL: Medium High       TEMP: 150°
MICROWAVE TIME: Approx. 30 min.

| | |
|---|---|
| 1½ lbs. ground chuck beef<br>3 slices fresh bread, cubed<br>1 cup milk<br>2 teaspoons salt<br>½ teaspoon pepper | Make meat loaf mixture: In large mixing bowl, mix together beef, bread cubes, milk, salt and pepper. |
| ½ cup chopped onion<br>¼ cup chopped green pepper<br>¼ cup chopped celery<br>2 tablespoons lemon juice<br>1 egg, slightly beaten<br>1 cup (4-oz.) shredded cheddar cheese<br>3 slices fresh bread, finely crumbled<br>1 tablespoon Worcestershire sauce | Make cheese stuffing: In 1½-qt. casserole place onion, pepper, celery and lemon juice. **Microwave at High 3 Minutes,** until tender crisp. Add egg to hot vegetables and stir to blend well. Stir in cheese and fine bread crumbs. |

To assemble meat loaf: Pat half of meat mixture in bottom of 9-in. pie plate. Mound filling over meat leaving about 1-in. uncovered at edges. On wax paper, pat remaining meat mixture into a 10-in. circle. Invert over filling, seal around edges. Brush assembled meat loaf with Worcestershire sauce.

Insert temperature probe so tip is in center of stuffing. Cover tightly with plastic wrap, arranging loosely around probe to vent. Attach cable end at receptacle. **Microwave at Medium High. Set Temp, Set 150°.**

When oven signals, remove meat loaf and let stand about 10 minutes to firm before serving. Serve in wedges.

Makes 4 to 6 servings

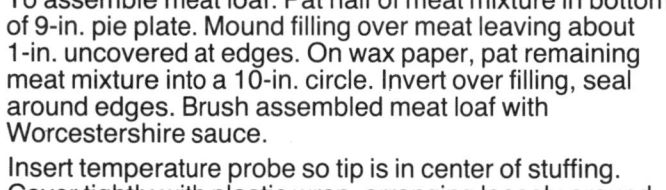

A 1½-lb. loaf shaped meat loaf can be microwaved at Medium High to 170°, in about 30 to 35 minutes.

**Plain meat loaf looks grey.** It needs a topping, sauce or browning agent for attractive color. For this picture we brushed the left side of the meat loaf with browning sauce, leaving the right side plain. Because microwave energy is attracted to sweet mixtures, toppings which contain sugar, syrup or preserves can increase over-browning if they come in contact with the bottom edges. When applied before microwaving, they should be brushed only on the top.

**Insert** temperature probe as horizontally as possible, so that tip is in the center of the loaf. Cover tightly with plastic wrap, arranging loosely around probe to vent.

## Basic Meat Loaf

*Add ¼ teaspoon herbs or dry mustard to vary flavor. You can make this recipe in a loaf shape by following the tip under the picture at left. Time will be extended by about 5 minutes, but some people prefer the loaf shape in order to make neat slices of leftover meat loaf for sandwiches.*

POWER LEVEL: High       TEMP: 170°
MICROWAVE TIME: 24 to 27 min.

| | |
|---|---|
| 1½ lbs. ground chuck beef<br>¾ cup chopped onion<br>½ cup fine dry bread crumbs<br>1 egg<br>2 tablespoons ketchup<br>⅔ cup milk<br>1 teaspoon salt<br>¼ teaspoon pepper<br>⅛ teaspoon paprika | Mix together beef, onion, crumbs, egg, ketchup, milk and seasonings. Mold into a rounded, flat loaf in 9-in. pie plate. |
| 2 tablespoons ketchup | Spread ketchup evenly over top of loaf. |

Insert temperature probe and cover with plastic wrap as shown in picture above. Attach cable end at receptacle. **Microwave at High. Set Temp, Set 170°.**

When oven signals, remove meat loaf and let stand about 10 minutes to firm before serving. Serve in wedges.

Make 6 servings

## Fruited Ham Slice

POWER LEVEL: High
MICROWAVE TIME: 20 to 21 min., total

| | |
|---|---|
| 1 small slice . . . . . . . . fully cooked ham, 1¼-in. thick (about 2-lbs.) | Score or remove fat from ham. Place ham slice in 8-in. square dish. Drain fruit, reserving juice. Arrange fruit attractively over ham slice. Cover with wax paper. **Microwave at High 10 Minutes.** Drain. |
| 1 can (11-oz.) mandarin orange segments | |
| 1 can (8¼-oz.) crushed pineapple | |
| Juice from fruits . . | Combine juice, sugar, cornstarch and cloves. **Microwave at High 5 to 6 Minutes** until thickened and clear. Pour carefully over ham slice to avoid disturbing the arranged fruit. Cover. **Microwave at High 5 Minutes,** until hot. Spoon sauce over fruit and serve. |
| 2 tablespoons brown sugar (packed) | |
| 2 teaspoons cornstarch | |
| ¼ teaspoon ground cloves | |

Makes 6 to 8 servings

## Classic Ham Loaf

POWER LEVEL: Medium   TEMP: 170°
MICROWAVE TIME: 10 to 23 min., total

| | |
|---|---|
| 1 lb. ground . . . . . . . cooked ham | Mix ground ham and pork thoroughly with crumbs, water, onion, and pepper. Press into 6-cup ring mold. |
| ½ lb. ground fresh pork | |
| ½ cup soft bread crumbs | |
| ½ cup water | Insert temperature probe so tip is in center of food. Cover tightly with plastic wrap, arranging loosely around probe to vent. Attach cable end at receptacle. **Microwave at Medium. Set Temp, Set 170°.** |
| 2 tablespoons instant minced onion | |
| ¼ teaspoon pepper | |

When oven signals, remove loaf from oven, and let stand 5 minutes before serving. Drain and invert onto serving platter. Spoon on glaze.

Makes 6 servings

**Glaze:** Stir 4 tablespoons apricot preserves until smooth; spoon and spread on hot ham loaf.

## Sweet and Sour Pork

POWER LEVEL: Medium and Medium High
MICROWAVE TIME: 50 min., total

| | |
|---|---|
| 1½ lbs. fresh pork, . . . . cut into 1-in. cubes | In 2-qt. casserole place pork, onion, soy sauce and browning sauce. Reserving juice, drain pineapple. Set aside. Add reserved juice to meat, stirring well. Cover. **Microwave at Medium 30 Minutes,** stirring after 15 minutes. |
| 1½ tablespoons instant minced onion | |
| 1 tablespoon soy sauce | |
| 1 teaspoon browning sauce | |
| 1 can (8¾-oz.) pineapple chunks | |
| 1 cup water . . . . . . . | In small bowl stir together water, vinegar, brown sugar, cornstarch and salt. Add to meat along with pineapple and water chestnuts. Cover. **Microwave at Medium High 20 Minutes,** stirring and adding green pepper after 10 minutes, until thickened and clear. |
| ¼ cup cider vinegar | |
| ¼ cup brown sugar (packed) | |
| 3 tablespoons cornstarch | |
| ½ teaspoon salt | |
| 1 can (5-oz.) water chestnuts, drained and sliced | |
| 1 medium green pepper, sliced in ½-in. strips | |
| 1 medium firm . . . . . . tomato, cut into chunks | Fold in tomato chunks and let stand, covered, 10 minutes before serving. Serve over rice or crisp noodles. |

Makes 6 servings

## Chili Pork Chops

POWER LEVEL: Medium
MICROWAVE TIME: 25 to 30 min., total

| | |
|---|---|
| 4 rib pork chops, . . . . 1-in. thick (1½ lbs.) | Score fat on chops and arrange in 8-in. square dish, so "tails" are in center. Place onion and green pepper slices on top of chops. Pour chili sauce over top. Cover with plastic wrap. **Microwave at Medium 25 to 30 Minutes,** rotating dish ½ turn after 15 minutes. |
| 4 onion slices, ¼-in. thick | |
| 4 green pepper rings, ¼ to ½-in. thick | |
| 1 bottle (12-oz.) chili sauce (1½ cups) | |

Makes 4 servings

## How to Microwave Lamb Roasts
Up to 3-lbs.

POWER LEVEL: Medium

13 to 14 Minutes Per Pound for Medium
15 to 16 Minutes Per Pound for Well done

**Microwaving by Temperature:** If desired, brush roast with diluted browning sauce. Place roast fat side down on trivet in 8-in. square dish. Insert temperature probe as directed below. Cover with wax paper.
**Microwave at Medium. Set Temp, Set 130°** for medium and **170°** for well done. Turn meat over when temperature reaches 90°. When oven signals, let stand 10 minutes before carving.
**Microwaving by Time:** Use minutes per pound, above. Turn meat over after about half the time. When oven signals, remove roast and insert conventional meat thermometer into roast in same location described for temperature probe. Check temperature after about 2 minutes; it should read 130° for medium and 170° for well done. If not, return to microwave oven a few minutes, then check again.
NOTE: Do not place conventional metal meat thermomenter in microwave oven.

## How to Microwave Veal Roasts
Up to 3-lbs.
*Microwaving works especially well on rolled and tied veal shoulder and other veal roasts.*

POWER LEVEL: Medium

16 to 18 Minutes Per Pound

If desired, brush roast with diluted browning sauce. Place roast fat side down in 8-in. square dish. Insert temperature probe as directed below. Cover with wax paper. **Microwave at Medium, Set Temp, Set 155°.** Turn meat over when temperature reaches 90°. When oven signals, let roast stand 10 minutes before carving.
**Microwaving By Time:** Use minutes per pound, above. Turn meat over after about half the time. When oven signals, remove roast and insert conventional meat thermometer into roast in same location as for temperature probe. Check temperature after about 2 minutes; it should read 155°. If not return to microwave oven a few minutes then check again.
NOTE: Do not place conventional metal meat thermometer in microwave oven.

## How to Insert the Temperature Probe
Measure the distance to the center of the roast by laying the temperature probe on top of the meat. If the roast is uneven in shape or contains fat or bone, select an angle which will bring the tip of the probe to the center of the thickest meaty area without touching fat or bone. Mark with your thumb and forefinger where the edge of the meat comes on the probe. Insert the probe up to the point marked with your finger.

## Microwaving Pork Roast by Time
Up to 3-lbs.

POWER LEVEL: Low
MICROWAVE TIME: 20 to 24 min., per lb.

Do not salt roast. Place bone side up in a 8-in. square dish. Add ¼ cup water. Cover with plastic wrap, or place in a cooking bag, fat side up.

Estimate the minimum total roasting time. **Microwave at Low.** Turn roast over after half of time. After minimum time, test internal temperature of the roast with a meat thermometer, following instructions given for probe placement. Allow 2 minutes for thermometer to register. If roast has not reached 170°, remove thermometer and return roast to the oven for a few more minutes.

When cooking is completed remove and let stand 20 minutes.

Note: Do not place conventional metal meat thermometer in microwave oven.

When cooking pork either conventionally or in the microwave oven, follow our directions exactly and always cook the meat to at least 170°. This assures that, in the remote possibility that trichina may be present it will be killed and the meat will be safe to eat.

## How to Cook Pork and Ham Roasts

POWER LEVEL: Medium

| ITEM | IN A COOKING BAG TIME/MIN., PER LB. | WITHOUT BAG, COVERED WITH PLASTIC WRAP TIME/MIN., PER LB. | COMMENTS |
|---|---|---|---|
| **Pork Loin or Rib,** (Up to 3 lbs.) | 15 to 17 | 16 to 19 | Roasts not cooked in a bag may be covered with plastic wrap, vented at one corner. Add ¼ cup water before covering. Microwave bone-side up first half of time. Pork should be cooked to 170°. Shield top edge of ham with a 1-in. wide strip of foil. |
| **Precooked: Canned, Butt or Shank** (Up to 3 lbs.) | —— | 9 to 12 | |

Be sure pork roasts are thoroughly defrosted before microwaving them.

## Crumb-Coated Chicken

POWER LEVEL: High
MICROWAVE TIME: 12 to 14 min., total

| | |
|---|---|
| 1 egg . . . . . . . . . . . . . .<br>¼ cup melted butter<br>½ teaspoon salt | In small bowl beat together egg, butter and salt. |
| ¾ cup buttery . . . . . flavored cracker crumbs (about 25)<br>1½ lbs. chicken pieces, skin removed | In shallow dish place crumbs. Coat chicken with crumbs, then egg mixture and crumbs again. In 8-in. square dish arrange chicken with meatiest pieces near edges of dish. Cover with wax paper. **Microwave at High 12 to 14 Minutes.** Rotate dish ½ turn after half the cooking time.<br><br>Makes 2 to 3 servings |

## Chicken 'n Dressing

POWER LEVEL: High
MICROWAVE TIME: 16 to 18 min., total

| | |
|---|---|
| 3 cups . . . . . . . . . . . . .<br>(½ 8-oz. pkg.)<br>herb seasoned stuffing mix<br>½ cup chopped celery<br>¼ cup minced onion<br>2 tablespoons chopped pimiento<br>1 egg<br>1 cup chicken broth | In 8-in. square dish combine stuffing mix, celery, onion, pimiento, egg and broth. |
| 1½ lbs. chicken . . . . . . pieces<br>2 tablespoons butter, melted<br>Salt<br>Paprika | Place chicken pieces on top of dressing with meaty pieces near edges of dish. Brush with melted butter, and sprinkle with salt and paprika. Cover with wax paper. |

**Microwave at High 16 to 18 Minutes.** Let stand about 5 minutes before serving.

Makes 2 to 3 servings

## Chicken in Italian Sauce

POWER LEVEL: High
MICROWAVE TIME: 25 to 27 min., total

| | |
|---|---|
| 2 whole chicken . . . . breasts, halved (1½ to 2 lbs.)<br>1 pkg. (1½-oz.) spaghetti sauce mix<br>½ cup water or dry white wine | In 8-in. square dish, arrange chicken breasts with thickest, meaty portions near edges of dish. Combine sauce mix and liquid; pour over top. Cover and **Microwave at High 15 Minutes,** until chicken is almost tender. |
| 2 tomatoes, . . . . . . . peeled and quartered<br>¼ lb. mushrooms, sliced | Stir tomatoes and mushrooms into chicken. **Microwave at High for 10 to 12 Minutes.** Serve over rice, if desired.<br><br>Makes 4 servings |

## Spanish Style Chicken

POWER LEVEL: High and Medium High
MICROWAVE TIME: 27 to 35 min., total

| | |
|---|---|
| 2 lbs. chicken . . . . . . pieces<br>1 teaspoon salt<br>¼ teaspoon pepper<br>¼ teaspoon chili powder<br>1 clove garlic, minced<br>⅛ teaspoon saffron powder<br>2 cups chicken broth<br>2 tablespoons sherry | In 8-in. square dish, place chicken with meaty pieces near edges. Sprinkle with salt, pepper, chili powder, garlic and saffron. Add broth and sherry. Cover. **Microwave at High 15 minutes.** Stir, recover and continue to **Microwave at Medium High 5 to 10 Minutes,** until chicken is tender. |
| 2 cups cooked . . . . . . . . rice<br>1 pkg. (10 oz.) frozen peas, defrosted<br>½ cup sliced stuffed green olives | Add cooked rice, peas and stuffed olives. Cover and **Microwave at High 7 to 10 Minutes** until vegetables are hot.<br><br>Makes 3 to 4 servings |

## Sweet 'n Tangy Chicken

POWER LEVEL: High
MICROWAVE TIME: 10 to 12 min., total

| | |
|---|---|
| 2 chicken breasts, . . halved, skinned and boned | In 8-in. square dish arrange chicken breasts with thickest, meaty portions near edges of dish. |
| 1 envelope . . . . . . . . . (1 serving size) instant onion soup mix<br>¼ cup bottled Russian dressing<br>½ cup apricot-pineapple preserves | In small bowl stir together, onion soup mix, dressing and preserves. Spread over chicken, coating each piece. Cover with wax paper. |

**Microwave at High 10 to 12 Minutes.** Rotate dish and spoon sauce over chicken after 6 minutes. Allow to stand 5 to 10 minutes before serving, so chicken absorbs flavor of sauce. Serve with rice, if desired.

Makes 4 servings

## Oriental Chicken

POWER LEVEL: High
MICROWAVE TIME: 7 to 10 min., total

| | |
|---|---|
| 2 chicken breasts, . . halved, skinned and boned | Cut chicken breasts into ½-in. wide strips; set aside. |
| ⅓ cup sherry . . . . . . . or rose wine<br>⅓ cup water<br>⅓ cup raisins<br>¼ cup soy sauce<br>2 tablespoons brown sugar<br>2 tablespoons cooking oil<br>1 tablespoon cornstarch<br>¼ teaspoon oregano<br>1 clove garlic, crushed | In 2-qt. casserole combine wine, water, raisins, soy sauce, brown sugar, oil, cornstarch, oregano and garlic. Cover. **Microwave at High 3 to 4 Minutes** until thick, stirring after 2 minutes. Stir in chicken strips. Cover and **Microwave at High 4 to 5 Minutes** or until done, stirring after 3 minutes. Serve with rice if desired.<br><br>Makes 4 servings |

## Mexican Chicken Casserole

POWER LEVEL: High        TEMP: 150°
MICROWAVE TIME: 20 to 24 minutes

| | |
|---|---|
| **1 can (10½-oz.)** . . . . **condensed cream of chicken soup**<br>**2 tablespoons green chilies, diced**<br>**¼ teaspoon instant minced onion**<br>**½ cup water** | In small mixing bowl place soup, chilies, onion and water. Stir until well blended. |
| **2 large, firm, ripe** . . . . **tomatoes** | Slice tomatoes in ½-in. slices. |
| **1 pkg. (6-oz.) corn** . . **chips**<br>**2 cups diced, cooked chicken, or 2 cans (5-oz. each) boned chicken, diced**<br>**1 cup (4-oz.) shredded cheddar cheese** | In 2-qt. casserole layer ½ of corn chips. Top with 1 cup chicken, then ½ of tomato slices. Pour ½ of soup mixture over chicken; sprinkle with ¾ of cheese, reserving rest for topping after cooking. Repeat layers. |

Insert temperature probe so tip is in center of casserole. Attach cable end at receptacle. Cover loosely with plastic wrap. **Microwave at High. Set Temp, Set 150°.** When oven signals, sprinkle with reserved cheese and let stand 5 minutes before serving.

Makes 6 to 8 servings

## Chicken à la King

*The old favorite, creamed chicken, dressed up with colorful pimiento, green pepper and flavorful mushrooms. Serve over toast or in a pastry shell.*

POWER LEVEL: High and Medium High
MICROWAVE TIME: 18 to 22 min., total

| | |
|---|---|
| **⅓ cup butter** . . . . . . . .<br>**⅓ cup unsifted all-purpose flour**<br>**2 cups dairy half & half**<br>**1 cup chicken broth** | In 2-qt. casserole place butter. Cover. **Microwave at High 2 Minutes,** until melted. Blend in flour. Gradually stir in half & half and broth; mix well. **Microwave at High 8 to 10 Minutes,** stirring with whisk after 4 minutes, until thickened and smooth. Stir well again. |
| **2 cups cubed,** . . . . . . **cooked chicken**<br>**1 jar (4-oz.) sliced pimiento**<br>**1 can (4-oz.) sliced mushrooms, undrained**<br>**½ cup diced green pepper**<br>**1 teaspoon salt**<br>**¼ teaspoon pepper** | Mix in chicken, pimiento, mushrooms, green pepper, salt and pepper. Cover. **Microwave at Medium High 8 to 10 Minutes,** until hot. Let stand 5 to 10 minutes before serving, to blend flavors. |

Makes 4 servings

## Brunswick Stew

*If a more highly seasoned stew is desired add 1 teaspoon Worcestershire sauce and 3 to 5 drops hot pepper (Tabasco) sauce.*

POWER LEVEL: Medium High and High
MICROWAVE TIME: 50 to 55 min., total

| | |
|---|---|
| **2 lbs. chicken** . . . . . . **pieces**<br>**1 cup water** | In 2-qt. casserole place chicken pieces and water. Cover. **Microwave at Medium High 20 to 25 Minutes,** until tender. Remove meat from bones discarding skin. Cut meat into pieces and set aside. |
| **2 cups diced raw** . . . . **potatoes (2 medium)**<br>**1 pkg. (10-oz.) frozen baby lima beans, defrosted**<br>**½ cup sliced onion (1 small)**<br>**1½ teaspoons salt**<br>**¼ teaspoon pepper** | Add potatoes, lima beans, onion, salt and pepper to casserole. **Microwave at Medium High 20 Minutes,** stirring after 10 minutes. |
| **1 can (12-oz.) whole** . . **kernel corn, undrained**<br>**¼ cup unsifted all-purpose flour**<br>**1 can (8-oz.) tomatoes** | Into small bowl drain liquid from corn and stir in flour, mixing well. Blend into hot mixture. Add corn, tomatoes and chicken. **Microwave at High 10 Minutes,** stirring after 5 minutes, until vegetables are hot and sauce is thickened. Let stand 5 to 10 minutes before serving, to blend flavors. |

Makes 4 to 6 servings

## Chicken in Wine

*Coq au Vin is its French name. This makes a delicious supper when served with rice and a salad.*

POWER LEVEL: Medium High and High
MICROWAVE TIME: 33 to 35 min., total

| | |
|---|---|
| **1 medium onion** . . . . **chopped (¾ cup)**<br>**2 lbs. chicken pieces**<br>**1 tablespoon paprika**<br>**2 tablespoons Minute tapioca**<br>**Sauce (below)** | In 2-qt. casserole, spread onion evenly. Arrange chicken with meaty pieces near edge of dish. Sprinkle with paprika and tapioca. Pour sauce (below) over all. Cover and **Microwave at Medium High 25 Minutes.** |
| **½ lb. large fresh** . . . . **mushrooms, quartered**<br>**1 tablespoon chopped parsley** | Add mushrooms and parsley and **Microwave at High for 8 to 10 Minutes** to heat. |

Makes 3 to 4 servings

**Sauce:** In small bowl stir together 1 cup white wine, ½ bay leaf, ½ teaspoon thyme, 1 teaspoon salt and ⅛ teaspoon freshly ground pepper.

When microwaving a whole chicken, be sure to select a young, plump tender bird. The skin should be smooth and have a pale, creamy color tinged with pink. If you are in doubt, choose a broiler-fryer. Avoid chickens with thick, bumpy skin and large amounts of bright yellow fat.

If you do not care to use a cooking bag, or if you prefer a drier surface, microwave chicken covered with wax paper. You may need to add 2 or more additional minutes per pound to the total cooking time. Microwaving chicken at Medium High rather than High eliminates excessive handling and foil for shielding.

## How to Microwave Whole Chicken in a Cooking Bag

POWER LEVEL:  Medium High
MICROWAVE TIME:   10 to 12 Minutes per lb.

**Brush** chicken with a mixture of 1 tablespoon bottled browning sauce and 1 tablespoon melted butter. Cut a ½-in. strip from open end of an oven cooking bag.

**Place** chicken in a bag on a microwave ovenproof platter or baking dish. Add ⅓ cup water, chicken broth or wine. Tie end of bag with plastic strip. Slash bag next to closure.

**Insert** temperature probe, if you are using it, through the bag into meatiest part of inner thigh, from below the end of and parallel to the leg. Microwave at Medium High to an internal temperature of 190°.

## Chicken Teriyaki

POWER LEVEL:  Medium High               TEMP: 190°
MICROWAVE TIME:   approx. 28 to 33 min., total

| | |
|---|---|
| ¼ cup soy sauce  . . . .<br>⅓ cup honey<br>⅓ cup sherry | In small cooking bag, mix soy sauce, honey and sherry. |
| 1 whole broiler-  . . . .<br>fryer, about 3-lbs. | Add chicken to bag and tie open end securely with plastic strip cut from open end of bag. |

Turn chicken on its side and place in 8-in. square dish. Marinate in refrigerator 1 to 2 hours, turning chicken over after ½ of time. To microwave, place bird breast side up in dish. Slash bag near closure. Insert temperature probe. **Microwave at Medium High. Set Temp, Set 190°.** When oven signals, remove chicken. Prepare Teriyaki Sauce (below) and finish chicken as described in sauce recipe.

Makes 4 servings

**Teriyaki Sauce:** In 1-qt. glass measuring cup stir together 2 tablespoons water and 1 tablespoon cornstarch. Cut off one corner of cooking bag with scissors and drain juices into cup. **Microwave at High 2 to 3 Minutes,** until thick and clear, stirring after 1 minute. After 10 minutes, remove chicken from bag to serving platter. Pour sauce over chicken just before serving.

## Barbecued Stuffed Chicken

POWER LEVEL:  Medium High
MICROWAVE TIME:  55 to 60 min., total

| | |
|---|---|
| 2 cups day-old  . . . . . .<br>½-in. bread cubes or<br>crumbled cornbread<br>¼ cup minced onion<br>¼ cup minced celery<br>1 teaspoon salt<br>1 teaspoon poultry<br>seasoning<br>¼ teaspoon pepper<br>3 tablespoons melted<br>butter<br>2 tablespoons<br>chicken broth or<br>water | In large bowl toss together bread, onion, celery, salt, poultry seasoning, pepper, butter and chicken broth to make stuffing. |
| 1 whole broiler-  . . . .<br>fryer, about 3-lbs.<br>¼ cup bottled<br>barbecue sauce | Fill body cavity of chicken with stuffing. Tie wings flat to body with string around chicken; tie legs together. Brush all areas with barbecue sauce. |

On trivet in 8-in. square dish place chicken with breast side down. Cover with wax paper. **Microwave at Medium High 55 to 60 Minutes,** turning chicken breast side up and brushing with barbecue sauce after 30 minutes. Chicken is done when no trace of pink shows in meat when cut is made between inner thigh and breast. Let chicken stand 10 minutes before serving.

Makes 4 servings

# 28 Poultry

Plain microwaved Cornish Hen in background contrasts with a hen brushed with teriyaki sauce before microwaving. Teriyaki sauce gives a more golden color than browning sauce, does.

## How to Defrost Cornish Hens

Delicate Cornish Hens need some extra attention during defrosting or they may start to cook. We recommend defrosting in 3 steps rather than 2.

POWER LEVEL: Defrost
MICROWAVE TIME: 6½ to 12 Minutes per lb.
(up to 3-lb.)

1. Place unwrapped poultry on trivet in microwave safe dish. **Microwave at Defrost** for ⅓ the total defrosting time.
2. Turn poultry over. **Microwave** for ⅓ of time.
3. Shield ends of legs, wing tips and warm areas with foil. **Microwave** for last ⅓ of time. If giblets do not move freely, run cold water into cavities.

## How to Microwave Cornish Hens

POWER LEVEL: High
MICROWAVE TIME: 8½ to 10 Minutes per lb.

1. Brush hens with browning sauce.
   Shield legs and wings with foil. Place breast side down on trivet in 8-in. square dish. Cover with wax paper. Microwave for ½ the cooking time.

2. Turn breast side up. Microwave for second ½ of time. Let stand 10 minutes to allow meat to firm. Test for doneness by piercing thigh with a fork; juice should run clear.

Rice is an excellent stuffing for Cornish Hens. For each hen use about ½ cup cooked rice (white and/or wild), well-buttered and seasoned. Or, stuff poultry with Fruited Rice Stuffing below.

## Fruited Rice Stuffing

*This recipe may be used to stuff a broiler-fryer chicken (about 3 pounds).*

POWER LEVEL: High
MICROWAVE TIME: 10 to 12 min., total

In 3-qt. casserole combine 2 cups packaged precooked (Minute) rice, 1 cup golden raisins, 1 cup finely diced celery, 1 small onion, chopped, 1¼ cups orange juice, 1 cup hot tap water, 2 tablespoons butter, 2 tablespoons grated orange peel, ½ teaspoon salt and ¼ teaspoon each pepper, thyme and marjoram. Cover. **Microwave at High for 10 to 12 Minutes,** stirring after 4 minutes. Cool.

Makes about 4 cups.

*Cornish Hens Stuffed with Long Grain and Wild Rice*

## Cornish Hens Far East Style

POWER LEVEL: High
MICROWAVE TIME: 23 to 26 min., total

| | |
|---|---|
| **2 cornish hens, each about 1-lb. defrosted** | Rinse hens; drain well. Place hens in heavy plastic bag in 8-in. square dish. |
| **¼ cup soy sauce** <br> **¼ cup sherry wine** <br> **¼ cup pineapple juice** <br> **1 clove garlic, crushed, or** <br> **⅛ teaspoon garlic powder** <br> **½ teaspoon curry powder** <br> **¼ teaspoon dry mustard** | In small bowl, mix together soy sauce; sherry, pineapple juice, garlic, curry powder and mustard. Pour over cornish hens in plastic bag. Squeeze bag to remove as much air as possible. Refrigerate 4 to 6 hours or overnight, turning occasionally. |

To cook, remove hens from plastic bag (reserve marinade). Place hens breast-side down on trivet in 8-in. square dish. Cover dish with wax paper. **Microwave at High 10 Minutes.** Turn hens breast-side up. Brush with marinade and rotate dish ½ turn. Recover. **Microwave at high 13 to 16 Minutes** more, until tender. If desired, split hens into halves. Serve immediately.

Makes 2 to 4 servings

## Hot Turkey and Cheese Sandwiches

*These are known in the South as "Hot Browns", created at a famous hotel in Louisville.*

POWER LEVEL: Medium High
MICROWAVE TIME: 12 to 14 min., total

| | |
|---|---|
| **4 strips bacon** ...... | On paper plate lined with double thickness paper towels, arrange bacon. Cover with single thickness paper towel. **Microwave at Medium High 2½ to 3 Minutes,** until only partially cooked. |
| **4 slices toast** ........<br>**8 to 12 large slices turkey breast (about ½ lb.)**<br>**4 slices tomato (½-in. thick)**<br>**1 recipe Cheese Sauce, page 34**<br>**4 teaspoons Parmesan cheese** | If necessary cut toast to fit bottom of 8-in. square dish. Arrange turkey on toast in dish. Top each toast slice with a tomato slice. Spoon cheese sauce over sandwiches. Sprinkle tops of sandwiches with Parmesan cheese. Arrange 2 slices partially-cooked bacon over each sandwich. |

Cover with wax paper. **Microwave at Medium High 9 to 11 Minutes,** until hot. Rotate dish after 5 minutes.

Makes 4 sandwiches

## Saucy Turkey and Broccoli

*Called Turkey Divan when made with the traditional Mornay Sauce. This makes a nice luncheon or supper dish. A salad of tomato slices is a colorful accompaniment.*

POWER LEVEL: High and Medium High
MICROWAVE TIME: 17 to 21½ min., total

| | |
|---|---|
| **1 bunch (about ...... 1¼-lb.) broccoli, quartered lengthwise and cut into 3½ to 4-in. long pieces** | In 8-in. square dish, arrange broccoli with "flowers" in center and stalks near edge of dish. Add ¼ cup water. Cover. **Microwave at High 5 to 6 Minutes** until almost tender. Drain. |
| **8 large slices ...... cooked turkey (about ½ lb.)**<br>**1 recipe Cheese Sauce, page 34** | Layer turkey slices over broccoli. Cover with sauce. **Microwave at Medium High 6 to 8 Minutes,** until hot. |

Makes 4 servings

*Hot Turkey and Cheese Sandwich*

## Turkey Tetrazzini

POWER LEVEL: High and Medium High
MICROWAVE TIME: 31 to 36 min., total

| | |
|---|---|
| **1 pkg. (7 to 8-oz.) .... spaghetti** | Cook spaghetti (see chart, page 13), except **Microwave at High 10 Minutes.** Drain. Place in greased 8-in. square dish. |
| **¼ cup butter** ........<br>**1 can (4-oz.) sliced mushrooms, drained**<br>**1 small onion, chopped**<br>**1½ teaspoons lemon juice** | In 2-qt. casserole place butter, mushrooms, onion and lemon juice. **Microwave at High 2 to 3 Minutes,** stirring after 1 minute. |
| **¼ cup flour** ..........<br>**1 teaspoon salt**<br>**½ teaspoon paprika**<br>**⅛ teaspoon nutmeg**<br>**2 cups turkey or chicken broth**<br>**½ cup dairy half & half** | Stir in flour, salt, paprika and nutmeg, until smooth. **Microwave at High 1 Minute.** Stir well, Gradually stir in broth and half & half. **Microwave at High 8 to 10 Minutes,** stirring every 2 minutes, until thickened. |
| **2½ cups cooked, .... cubed turkey**<br>**½ cup grated Parmesan cheese paprika** | Mix in turkey. Pour over spaghetti. Sprinkle with cheese and paprika. **Microwave at Medium High 10 to 12 Minutes,** until hot. |

Makes 4 to 6 servings

## Scalloped Fish or Scallops

POWER LEVEL: High
MICROWAVE TIME: 10 to 11 min., total

| | |
|---|---|
| **1 lb. white fish fillets or scallops** | On microwave ovenproof platter or 9-in. pie plate place fish fillets or scallops with thickest portions near edges of dish. Cover with dampened paper towel which has most of water squeezed out. **Microwave at High 4 Minutes.** Remove platter from oven and let stand covered with paper towel while preparing buttered crumbs. |
| **½ cup (¼-lb.) butter** <br> **1 cup soft bread crumbs** <br> **1 cup saltine cracker crumbs** | In 1-qt. glass measure place butter. **Microwave at High 2 Minutes,** or until melted. Add bread and cracker crumbs. Mix with fork. |
| **1 teaspoon salt** <br> **⅛ teaspoon freshly ground pepper** <br> **⅓ cup milk or cream** | Remove paper towel from fish and sprinkle evenly with salt and pepper, then buttered crumbs. Pour milk evenly over top. **Microwave at High 4 to 5 Minutes** more. |

Makes 4 servings

## Tuna Noodle Casserole

POWER LEVEL: High
MICROWAVE TIME: 29 to 33 min., total

| | |
|---|---|
| **1 pkg. (8-oz.) narrow egg noodles** | Microwave noodles (see chart, page 13), except **Microwave at High 5 Minutes.** |
| **3 tablespoons butter** <br> **1 clove garlic, minced** <br> **½ cup finely chopped green onions** <br> **½ teaspoon salt** <br> **⅛ teaspoon pepper** | In 2-qt. casserole place butter, garlic, onion, salt and pepper. **Microwave at High 3 to 4 Minutes,** stirring after 1 minute, until onion is softened. |
| **2 tablespoons all-purpose flour** <br> **1½ cups milk** | Stir in flour until smooth. Gradually stir in milk. **Microwave at High 6 to 7 Minutes,** stirring every 2 minutes, until smooth and thickened. |
| **2 cans (7-oz. each) tuna, drained and flaked** | Gently stir tuna and noodles into sauce. Cover. **Microwave at High 15 to 17 Minutes,** stirring after 8 minutes, until hot. |
| **⅓ cup cracker crumbs** <br> **2 tablespoons minced parsley** <br> **2 tablespoons melted butter** | In small bowl, mix together crumbs, parsley and butter. Sprinkle over casserole before serving. |

Makes 6 to 8 servings

## Dilled Salmon Steaks

POWER LEVEL: High
MICROWAVE TIME: 6 to 8 min., total

| | |
|---|---|
| **4 small (½-in. thick) salmon steaks (1-lb.)** <br> **2 tablespoons melted butter** <br> **2 teaspoons lemon juice** <br> **½ teaspoon dill weed** | In paper towel lined 8-in. square dish place steaks. Brush with melted butter mixed with lemon juice. Sprinkle with dill. Cover dish with wax paper. |

**Microwave at High 6 to 8 Minutes.** When done, fish will flake easily with fork. Turn fish over onto serving plate. (Paper towel absorbs juices for best appearance of fish.) Garnish top of steaks with sprinkling of paprika or parsley and additional melted butter, if desired.

Makes 4 servings

## Fillets in Lemon Butter

POWER LEVEL: High
MICROWAVE TIME: 8 to 10 min., total

| | |
|---|---|
| **1 lb. firm fish fillets** <br> **½ to 1 teaspoon salt** <br> **⅛ teaspoon pepper** | Sprinkle fish fillets with salt and pepper. Starting at tail end, roll fillets up. Arrange rolls in 8-in. square dish. |
| **½ cup (¼-lb.) butter** <br> **3 tablespoons chopped parsley** <br> **1 tablespoon lemon juice** <br> **½ cup buttery flavored cracker crumbs** <br> **½ teaspoon paprika** | In 1-qt. glass measure place butter. **Microwave at High 2 Minutes,** until melted. Blend in parsley and lemon juice and pour over fish rolls. Top with crumbs then sprinkle on paprika. **Microwave at High 6 to 8 Minutes.** Rotate dish ½ turn after half of cooking. |

Makes 4 servings

## Scalloped Tuna and Chips

POWER LEVEL: High
MICROWAVE TIME: 23 to 25 min., total

| | |
|---|---|
| **1 can (10½-oz.) condensed cream of celery soup** <br> **1 can (7 to 8-oz.) mushroom stems and pieces** <br> **1 teaspoon instant minced onion** <br> **1 tablespoon chopped parsley** <br> **1 cup milk** <br> **1 tablespoon lemon juice** | Mix soup, undrained mushrooms, onion, parsley, milk and lemon juice. |
| **3 cups crushed potato chips** <br> **2 cans (7-oz. each) tuna, drained and flaked** | In 2-qt. greased casserole layer 1 cup crushed chips, ½ of tuna, ½ of soup mixture. Repeat layers and top with potato chips. **Microwave at High 23 to 25 Minutes,** until bubbly. |

Makes 6 servings

## Shrimp Gumbo

*For spicy flavor, tie 1 to 2 teaspoons crab boil in a cheesecloth bag and add along with shrimp. For bright color accent, save about ¼ of green pepper to stir into finished gumbo.*

POWER LEVEL: High
MICROWAVE TIME: 36 to 38 min., total

| | |
|---|---|
| 1 cup diced green pepper (2 medium) <br> 1 medium onion, sliced (about ½ cup) <br> 2 cloves garlic, crushed <br> ¼ cup butter (use bacon fat, if desired) | In 2-qt. casserole place green pepper, onion, garlic and butter. **Microwave at High 8 Minutes,** stirring every 3 minutes, until onion is tender. |
| 1 tablespoon cornstarch <br> 1 cup water <br> 1 can (14½ to 16-oz.) stewed tomatoes <br> 1½ teaspoons salt <br> ½ teaspoon ground nutmeg <br> ¼ teaspoon pepper <br> 1 pkg. (10-oz.) frozen okra, defrosted, cut into 1-in. pieces | In small bowl stir together cornstarch and water. Add to onion along with tomatoes, salt, nutmeg, pepper, and okra. Stir well. Cover. **Microwave at High 25 Minutes,** stirring and recovering after ½ of time. |
| 1 pound fresh shrimp, shelled, deveined | Add shrimp. Cover and **Microwave at High 3 to 5 Minutes,** just until shrimp are firm. |

Makes 4 to 6 servings

## Scalloped Oysters

POWER LEVEL: High
MICROWAVE TIME: 20 to 22 min., total

| | |
|---|---|
| 3 cans (12-oz. each) frozen oysters, thawed (about 4 cups) | Drain oysters, reserving ¼ cup liquid. |
| ¾ cup butter, melted <br> 2 cups fine soda cracker crumbs (about 40 small squares) <br> 1 teaspoon salt <br> ⅛ teaspoon pepper <br> ⅛ teaspoon nutmeg | In small mixing bowl mix together butter and crumbs. In 8-in. square dish, layer ⅔ cup of crumb mixture, ½ of drained oysters, ½ of seasonings, then ⅔ cup crumbs, rest of oysters, seasonings and crumbs. |
| ¼ cup milk | Mix milk with oyster liquid and pour evenly over top. |

With knife, poke 3 to 4 holes through layers so liquid goes to bottom. **Microwave at High 8 Minutes.** Sprinkle with ¼ cup chopped parsley. Rotate dish ½ turn. **Microwave 12 to 14 Minutes,** until oysters are firm when pierced with fork.

Makes about 6 servings

## Creamed Scallops

*The classic dish often known as Coquille St. Jacques. Large scallop shells are natural microwave utensils.*

POWER LEVEL: High and Medium
MICROWAVE TIME: 20 to 24 min., total

| | |
|---|---|
| 3 tablespoons butter <br> 1 jar (4-oz.) sliced mushrooms, drained <br> 2 green onions, sliced <br> ¼ cup chopped celery | In 2-qt. casserole place butter, mushrooms, onions and celery. **Microwave at High 5 Minutes,** stirring after 2 minutes. |
| 2 tablespoons flour <br> ½ teaspoon salt <br> ¼ teaspoon thyme <br> 1 tablespoon pimiento, chopped <br> ⅓ cup white wine <br> 1 lb. raw scallops | Stir in flour, salt, thyme and pimiento well, then wine and scallops, stirring again. **Microwave at High 5 to 6 Minutes,** stirring after 3 minutes until thickened. |
| ¼ cup dairy half & half <br> 1 egg yolk, beaten | Stir in half & half and egg yolk. **Microwave at Medium 3 to 4 Minutes,** stirring after 2 minutes. |

Spoon mixture into 6 scallop shells or small dishes. Top with Crumb Mixture (below). Place 3 shells at a time in microwave oven. Cover with wax paper. **Microwave at Medium High 3 to 4 Minutes,** rearranging after 2 minutes, until hot. Repeat.

Makes 6 servings

**Crumb Mixture:** In small bowl, place 2 tablespoons butter. **Microwave at High 1 Minute,** until melted. Stir in ¼ cup fine dry bread crumbs and 2 tablespoons Parmesan cheese.

## Sweet and Sour Shrimp

*Garnish with chopped bacon and green onion slices, if desired.*

POWER LEVEL: High
MICROWAVE TIME: 3 to 8 min., total

| | |
|---|---|
| 1 recipe Sweet and Sour Sauce, (page 34) <br> 1 lb. cleaned and cooked shrimp <br> 1 can (8-oz.) pineapple slices, drained | Stir together Sweet and Sour Sauce, shrimp and drained pineapple slices. **Microwave at High 3 to 8 Minutes,** or until hot, stirring gently after 3 minutes. |

Makes 4 servings

Eggs microwave rapidly, and since they are a delicate food, toughen when overcooked. The yolks, which have a higher fat content, cook faster than the whites. When yolks and whites are mixed together, eggs may be cooked at higher power setting. Omelets, which need time to set, are cooked at Medium, while scrambled eggs, which are stirred, are microwaved at Medium High. Scrambled eggs are one of many foods which microwave better than they cook conventionally.

## Eggs Benedict

POWER LEVEL: High
MICROWAVE TIME: 13 to 14 min., total

| | |
|---|---|
| **4 poached eggs** .... **(page 11)** | Poach eggs and allow to stand as directed. |
| **2 egg yolks** ......... **1 tablespoon lemon juice** **½ teaspoon dry mustard** **⅛ teaspoon salt** **½ cup (¼-lb.) butter** | While eggs are standing, make Hollandaise Sauce. In container of electric blender measure egg yolks, lemon juice, mustard and salt. In 1-qt. glass measure place butter. **Microwave at High 1½ to 2 Minutes** until hot and bubbly. Turn electric blender to highest speed and gradually add butter, blending until creamy and thickened. |
| **8 thin slices (¼-in.** .. **thick) Canadian bacon** | Just before serving, microwave Canadian bacon which has been arranged in single layer on microwave safe plate. **Microwave at High 2 Minutes.** |
| **4 English muffins,** .. **split and toasted** | Assemble Eggs Benedict by arranging 2 slices of Canadian bacon, then a poached egg over each of 4 English muffin halves. Top eggs with Hollandaise Sauce. Butter remaining muffin halves and serve as accompaniment. |

Makes 4 servings

## Cheese Fondue with Natural Cheese

*It is important to whisk or stir the fondue every minute.*

POWER LEVEL: High and Medium
MICROWAVE TIME: 11 to 12 min., total

| | |
|---|---|
| **1 cup dry white wine** **2 tablespoons kirsch (optional)** | .. In 2-qt. microwave safe fondue pot or casserole place wine and kirsch. **Microwave at High 5 Minutes.** |
| **5 cups (20-oz.)** ...... **shredded gruyere cheese or Swiss cheese** **3 tablespoons flour** **⅛ teaspoon pepper** **Dash nutmeg** | Toss cheese with flour, pepper and nutmeg, until coated. Stir into hot wine. Cover **Microwave at Medium 6 to 7 Minutes,** stir briskly every minute, until melted. Serve with cubes of crusty bread. |

Makes about 4 servings

## Fluffy Cheese Omelet

POWER LEVEL: High and Medium
MICROWAVE TIME: 7½ to 10 min., total

| | |
|---|---|
| **3 eggs, separated** .. **⅓ cup mayonnaise** **2 tablespoons water** | In large mixer bowl beat egg whites at highest speed of mixer, until soft peaks form. Then in smaller bowl, using same beaters, beat yolks, mayonnaise and water. Gently pour yolk mixture over beaten whites. Fold together carefully. |
| **2 tablespoons** ...... **butter** | In 9-in. pie plate place butter. **Microwave at High 1 Minute,** swirl to coat dish. Carefully pour egg mixture into pie plate. **Microwave at Medium 6 to 8 Minutes.** |
| **½ cup finely** ....... **shredded cheddar cheese** | Sprinkle cheese over omelet. |

**Microwave at Medium ½ to 1 Minute,** until cheese is slightly melted. Quickly run spatula or turner around sides and bottom of dish. Fold half of omelet over the other half. Gently slide onto serving plate. Sprinkle with chives, if desired.

Makes 1 to 2 servings

**Jelly Omelet variation: Microwave** ¼ to ⅓ cup jelly **at High 1 to 2 Minutes,** until jelly is soft and can be stirred smooth. Set aside. Follow Fluffy Omelet recipe above **omitting** cheese and mayonnaise. Spoon jelly over half of omelet when set but still glossy on top. Fold plain half of omelet over jelly half. If desired, sprinkle cinnamon-sugar over omelet before serving.

Makes 1 to 2 servings

## Cheese Rarebit

POWER LEVEL: High and Medium
MICROWAVE TIME: 5 to 7 min., total

| | |
|---|---|
| **8 oz. pasteurized** .... **processed cheese, cubed** **1 tablespoon butter** | In 1-qt. casserole place cheese and butter. **Microwave at High 2 to 3 Minutes,** stirring every minute, until smooth. |
| **¼ teaspoon salt** .... **¼ teaspoon dry mustard** **½ teaspoon Worcestershire sauce** **Dash cayenne pepper** **¼ cup dairy half & half** **1 egg yolk, beaten** | Add salt, mustard, Worcestershire sauce and cayenne pepper. Quickly stir in half & half and egg yolk. **Microwave at Medium 3 to 4 Minutes,** stirring every minute, until hot. Serve over toast. |

Makes 3 to 4 servings

## Classic Quiche Lorraine

POWER LEVEL: High, Medium High and Medium
MICROWAVE TIME: 14 to 18 min., total

| | |
|---|---|
| 6 strips crisp . . . . . . . . . cooked bacon, crumbled | Reserve 2 tablespoons each of bacon and cheese and 1 tablespoon onion. Sprinkle remaining bacon, cheese and onion over bottom of microwaved pastry crust. |
| ½ cup grated Swiss cheese | |
| 3 green onions, chopped | |
| 1 Quiche Pastry, pg. 43 | |
| 1½ tablespoons flour . . | In 1-qt. measure mix flour, salt, nutmeg and cayenne. Gradually stir in milk and cream. **Microwave at High 7 to 8 Minutes.** Stir every 2 minutes. |
| ¼ teaspoon salt | |
| ¼ teaspoon nutmeg Dash cayenne | |
| 1 cup milk | |
| 1 cup whipping cream | |
| 4 eggs . . . . . . . . . . . . . . | In 1-qt. casserole beat eggs. Stir in hot liquid. |

**Microwave at Medium High 2 to 3 Minutes,** stirring every ½ minute, until thick. Pour into pastry. Top with bacon, cheese, onion and, if desired, paprika. **Microwave at Medium 5 to 7 Minutes,** until almost set. Let stand 5 minutes.

Makes 1 (9-in.) quiche, about 6 servings

## Cheese Enchiladas

POWER LEVEL: High and Medium High
MICROWAVE TIME: 19 to 20 min., total

| | |
|---|---|
| 1 cup ricotta cheese . . | In mixing bowl stir together ricotta, egg, onions, chilies, cumin and Monterey Jack cheese. |
| 1 egg | |
| ½ cup chopped green onions | |
| 2 tablespoons chopped green chilies | |
| 1 teaspoon cumin | |
| 1 cup (4-oz.) shredded Monterey Jack cheese | |
| 6 fresh corn or flour . . tortillas, (about 6-in. diameter) or, canned tortillas (5-in. diameter) | Wrap tortillas in moist paper towels. **Microwave at High 2 Minutes,** until pliable. Divide filling among tortillas. Roll up each one tightly. |
| 1 can (10-oz.) . . . . . . . . enchilada sauce | In lightly greased 8-in. square dish place rolls, seam side down. Pour sauce over rolls. **Microwave at Medium High 15 Minutes.** |
| 1 cup (4-oz.) . . . . . . . . . shredded cheddar cheese | Cover with cheddar cheese. **Microwave at High 2 to 3 Minutes,** until cheese is almost melted. |
| Sour cream and . . . . chopped green onions | Garnish with sour cream and green onions. |

Makes 2 to 4 servings

## Golden Onion Quiche

POWER LEVEL: High and Medium
MICROWAVE TIME: 16 to 18 min., total

| | |
|---|---|
| 1 commercially . . . . . . frozen pie crust  Worcestershire sauce (about 2 teaspoons) | Remove pastry from foil pan to glass 8-in. pie plate. **Microwave at High 1 Minute,** until softened. With fingers, press firmly in pie plate. Brush inside with Worcestershire sauce. Prick pastry. **Microwave at High 5 Minutes.** Rotate dish ¼ turn after 3 minutes. |
| 1 cup (4-oz.) . . . . . . . . . . shredded mozzarella or pizza cheese | Sprinkle cheese over bottom of pie shell. |
| 3 eggs . . . . . . . . . . . . . . . ½ cup whipping cream 3 drops hot pepper sauce (Tabasco) | With fork, beat together eggs, cream and hot pepper sauce. Pour over cheese in pie shell. |
| 1 can (2.8-oz.) . . . . . . . . French fried onions | With sharp knife, cut through onions in can to chop medium fine. Pour over top and lightly press down. |
| 1 tablespoon dried . . . . or frozen chives, or chopped green onion | Sprinkle chives or onion over top. |

**Microwave at Medium 10 to 12 Minutes.** Let stand about 5 minutes to firm slightly before serving.

Makes 1 (8-in.) pie, about 6 servings.

*Golden Onion Quiche*

## Basic White Sauce

POWER LEVEL: High
MICROWAVE TIME: 6 to 7½ min., total

| | |
|---|---|
| **2 tablespoons butter**<br>**2 tablespoons flour**<br>**½ teaspoon salt** | In 1-qt. glass measure place butter, flour and salt. **Microwave at High 2 Minutes,** stirring after 1 minute. |
| **1 cup milk** ......... | Gradually stir in milk. **Microwave at High 4 to 5½ Minutes,** stirring every minute until thick and bubbly. For thicker sauce, use 3 tablespoons flour instead of 2 tablespoons. |

Makes 1 cup

**Cheese Sauce Variation:** Add 1 cup (4-oz.) shredded sharp cheese and a dash of cayenne pepper to White Sauce. Stir to melt cheese after microwaving as directed above.

## Classic Italian Sauce

POWER LEVEL: High
MICROWAVE TIME: 23 to 25 min., total

| | |
|---|---|
| **1 large onion, chopped**<br>**3 tablespoons olive or cooking oil**<br>**3 cloves garlic, minced** | In 2-qt. casserole place onion, oil and garlic. **Microwave at High 5 Minutes,** stirring after 2 minutes, until onion is tender. |
| **2 cans (15-oz. each) tomato sauce**<br>**2 cans (6-oz. each) tomato paste**<br>**⅔ cup burgundy or tomato juice**<br>**2 tablespoons brown sugar (packed)**<br>**2 teaspoons Worcestershire sauce**<br>**1 teaspoon oregano**<br>**1 teaspoon basil**<br>**1 teaspoon salt**<br>**½ teaspoon pepper** | Add tomato sauce, tomato paste, wine or juice, brown suagr, Worcestershire sauce, oregano, basil, salt and pepper. Mix together well. Cover. **Microwave at High 18 to 20 Minutes,** stirring every 5 minutes, until very hot. |

Makes about 1½ quarts

## Barbecue Sauce

POWER LEVEL: High
MICROWAVE TIME: 9 to 10 min., total

| | |
|---|---|
| **1 cup chili sauce** ....<br>**½ cup water**<br>**¼ cup lemon juice**<br>**1 tablespoon cooking oil**<br>**2 tablespoons brown sugar (packed)**<br>**½ teaspoon salt**<br>**¼ teaspoon paprika**<br>**¼ teaspoon hot pepper sauce**<br>**1 tablespoon Worcestershire sauce** | In 1-qt. casserole thoroughly combine chili sauce, water, lemon juice, cooking oil, brown sugar, salt, paprika, hot pepper sauce and Worcestershire sauce. Cover. **Microwave at High 9 to 10 Minutes,** stirring after 3 minutes, until hot. |

Makes 2 cups

## Clam Sauce

POWER LEVEL: High
MICROWAVE TIME: 7 to 9 min., total

| | |
|---|---|
| **2 tablespoons olive oil**<br>**3 cloves garlic, minced**<br>**¼ teaspoon salt** | In 1-qt. casserole place oil, garlic and salt. **Microwave at High 2 Minutes,** until garlic clove becomes soft. |
| **2 cans (6.5-oz. each) minced clams**<br>**¼ cup water**<br>**1 tablespoon cornstarch**<br>**¼ cup minced parsley** | Drain clams, reserving juice. Set aside. Stir together water and cornstarch. Add to garlic along with clam juice and parsley. **Microwave at High 4 to 5 Minutes,** stirring after 2 minutes, until thickened. Stir in clams. **Microwave at High 1 to 2 Minutes,** until hot. |

Makes about 2 cups

## Sweet and Sour Sauce

POWER LEVEL: High
MICROWAVE TIME: 8 to 9 min., total

| | |
|---|---|
| **½ cup sugar** .......<br>**2 tablespoons cornstarch**<br>**¼ cup cold water** | In 1½-qt. casserole stir together sugar, cornstarch and water, until well blended. |
| **1 can (8-oz.) crushed pineapple**<br>**½ cup chopped green pepper**<br>**¼ cup (2-oz. can) chopped pimiento**<br>**½ clove garlic, minced**<br>**½ cup cider vinegar**<br>**2 tablespoons soy sauce**<br>**10 drops hot pepper sauce (Tabasco)** | Stir in pineapple, green pepper, pimiento, garlic, vinegar, soy sauce and hot pepper sauce. **Microwave at High 8 to 9 Minutes,** stirring every 2 minutes, until clear and thickened. Let sauce stand 5 to 10 minutes, to develop flavor, before serving. |

Makes about 1¾ cups

## Creamy Horseradish Sauce

POWER LEVEL: High
MICROWAVE TIME: 5 to 6 min., total

| | |
|---|---|
| **1 egg** ..............<br>**1½ cups milk**<br>**2 tablespoons cornstarch**<br>**2 tablespoons powdered horseradish**<br>**¼ cup vinegar**<br>**1 tablespoon sugar** | In 1½-qt. casserole, beat egg with milk. Stir in cornstarch, horseradish, vinegar, and sugar. **Microwave at High 5 to 6 Minutes.** |
| **2 tablespoons butter** ...... | Stir in butter. Serve with roast beef sandwiches. |

Makes about 2 cups

## Jiffy Spanish Rice

POWER LEVEL: High
MICROWAVE TIME: 17 to 19 min., total

| | |
|---|---|
| 1 lb. ground chuck .. beef | In 2-qt. casserole crumble beef. **Microwave at High 6 to 7 Minutes,** stirring after 3 minutes. Drain. Add rice, tomatoes, onion, chili powder, salt and pepper. Cover. **Microwave at High 11 to 12 Minutes.** Stir well. Let stand, covered, about 5 to 10 minutes before serving. |
| 1 cup packaged precooked (Minute) rice | |
| 1 can (1-lb. 12-oz.) tomatoes, undrained, cut up | |
| 1 tablespoon instant minced onion | |
| 1 or 2 tablespoons chili powder | |
| 2 teaspoons salt | |
| 1/8 teaspoon pepper | Makes 4 to 6 servings |

## Creamy Macaroni and Cheese

POWER LEVEL: High and Medium High
MICROWAVE TIME: 23 to 28 min., total

| | |
|---|---|
| 1 pkg. (7 to 8-oz.) .... elbow macaroni | Cook macaroni (see chart page 13), except **Microwave at High 9 Minutes.** Drain well and return to same casserole. |
| 1/4 cup butter ........ | In 1-qt. measure place butter. **Microwave at High 1 1/2 Minute,** to melt. |
| 6 tablespoons ...... flour | Blend in flour and salt. Stir in milk until smooth. **Microwave at High 5 1/2 to 7 Minutes,** stirring with wire whisk every minute, until thickened. |
| 1 teaspoon salt | |
| 2 cups milk | |
| 2 cups (8-oz.)........ grated sharp cheddar cheese | Stir in cheese until completely melted. |

Stir sauce into drained macaroni, mixing well. **Microwave at Medium High 7 to 10 Minutes,** stirring after 4 minutes. If desired, sprinkle top with paprika or buttered crumbs before serving.

Makes 6 to 8 servings

**Quick and Easy Macaroni and Cheese variation:** Omit sauce ingredients from above recipe. To cooked macaroni add 1 lb. pkg. processed cheese, cubed, and 1 can (5 1/3 oz.) evaporated milk. **Microwave at High 6 to 8 Minutes.** Stir and serve.

Makes 6 to 8 servings

## Grits and Cheese Casserole

POWER LEVEL: High and Medium
MICROWAVE TIME: 22 min., total

| | |
|---|---|
| 2 cups hot tap ...... water | In 1 1/2-qt. casserole place water, grits and salt. **Microwave at High 10 Minutes,** uncovered, stirring after 6 minutes. |
| 1/2 cup quick grits | |
| 1/2 teaspoon salt | |
| 3 tablespoons ...... butter, sliced | Add butter and cheese to grits. Mix well. **Microwave at High 2 Minutes,** until melted, stirring well. |
| 4 oz. pasteurized processed cheese, cubed | |
| 2 eggs, beaten ...... milk | In 1-cup measure beat eggs and fill to 3/4 cup line with milk. Add garlic powder and pepper sauce. Quickly stir into grits. |
| 1/8 teaspoon garlic powder | |
| Dash hot pepper sauce (Tabasco) | |
| 3/4 cup coarsely ...... crushed corn flakes | Sprinkle corn flakes over top. Dot with butter. Sprinkle with paprika. **Microwave at Medium 10 Minutes,** until set. Let stand 10 minutes. Especially good with ham. |
| 1 tablespoon butter paprika | |

Makes 6 servings

## Spaghetti-Cheese Casserole

POWER LEVEL: High
MICROWAVE TIME: 17 to 19 min., total

| | |
|---|---|
| 1 pkg. (7 to 8-oz.) .... spaghetti | Cook spaghetti (see chart page 13), except **Microwave at High 9 Minutes.** |
| 1 can (10 1/2-oz.) ...... condensed cream of mushroom soup | In small bowl mix soup, milk, onion, pepper and olives. |
| 1/2 cup milk | |
| 1 teaspoon instant minced onion | |
| 1/8 teaspoon pepper | |
| 1/2 cup sliced stuffed olives | |
| 2 cups (8-oz.) ........ shredded cheddar cheese | In greased 1 1/2-qt. casserole, layer half of spaghetti, cheese and soup mixture. Repeat layers. **Microwave at High 8 to 10 Minutes,** rotating dish 1/4 turn after 4 minutes. |

Makes 4 to 6 servings

## Ripe Olive Risotto

*Risotto means rice casserole. This combination is colorful with olives and pimiento.*

POWER LEVEL: High
MICROWAVE TIME: 22 to 26 min., total

| | |
|---|---|
| ¼ **cup butter or** ...... **cooking oil**<br>1 **cup finely chopped onion**<br>⅓ **cup chopped celery**<br>1 **cup uncooked long grain rice**<br>2 **cups chicken bouillon**<br>1 **teaspoon salt**<br>¼ **teaspoon pepper** | In 2-qt. casserole combine butter, onion, celery, rice, bouillon, salt and pepper. Cover. **Microwave at High 20 to 22 Minutes,** stirring after 10 minutes. |
| ½ **cup chopped ripe** .. **olives**<br>1 **can (4-oz.) mushroom stems and pieces, drained**<br>1 **jar (2-oz.) pimiento strips**<br>¼ **cup grated Parmesan cheese** | Add olives, mushrooms, pimiento and cheese. Stir to mix well. **Microwave at High 2 to 4 Minutes.** Stir before serving. |

Makes 6 to 8 servings

*Green Rice Casserole*

## Noodles Romanoff

POWER LEVEL: High
MICROWAVE TIME: 19 to 22 min., total

| | |
|---|---|
| 1 **pkg. (7 to 8-oz.)** .... **narrow noodles** | Cook noodles (see chart, page 13), except only **Microwave at High 8 Minutes.** Place in 2-qt. casserole. |
| 1 **cup cottage** ...... **cheese**<br>1 **cup (8-oz.) dairy sour cream**<br>½ **cup chopped stuffed green olives**<br>1 **teaspoon instant minced onion**<br>½ **teaspoon salt**<br>½ **teaspoon Worcestershire sauce**<br>**Dash hot pepper sauce (Tabasco)** | Add cheese, sour cream, olives, onion, salt, Worcestershire sauce and hot pepper sauce. Mix well. Cover. **Microwave at High 8 to 10 Minutes,** until hot. |
| 1 **cup (4-oz.)** ........ **shredded sharp cheese, or grated Parmesan cheese** | Sprinkle cheese on top. **Microwave at High 3 to 4 Minutes** more, uncovered. |

Makes 6 servings

## Green Rice Casserole

POWER LEVEL: High and Medium
MICROWAVE TIME: 23 to 27 min., total

| | |
|---|---|
| 1 **pkg. (10-oz.)** ...... **frozen chopped spinach** | Place spinach in a 2-qt. casserole. **Microwave at High 8 to 9 Minutes.** Drain well and set aside. |
| 1 **can (13-oz.)** ...... **evaporated milk**<br>⅔ **cup package precooked (Minute) rice**<br>1 **pkg. (8-oz.) pasteurized processed cheese, cubed**<br>¼ **cup chopped onion**<br>½ **teaspoon salt**<br>¼ **teaspoon pepper** | In same casserole, mix milk, rice, cheese, onion, salt and pepper. Cover. **Microwave at High 7 to 8 Minutes,** stirring every 2 minutes until cheese melts. |
| 3 **eggs, beaten** ...... | Add eggs and spinach to rice mixture and pour into an 8-cup ring mold or casserole. Cover with wax paper. **Microwave at Medium 8 to 10 Minutes** until center is set, rotating ¼ turn every 3 minutes. |

Makes 6 to 8 servings

## Eggplant Italiano

*This hearty vegetable casserole goes well with plain meats such as roasts, lamb, ham or chicken.*

POWER LEVEL: Medium High and High
MICROWAVE TIME: 23 to 26 min., total

| | |
|---|---|
| 1 medium .......... eggplant (1¼ lb.) | Pare eggplant: slice ⅛-in. thick. |
| 2 cans (8-oz. each) .. tomato sauce<br>1 to 2 teaspoons oregano<br>½ cup shredded sharp cheese (optional) | Spread 2 tablespoons tomato sauce in bottom of 2-qt. casserole. Layer half of eggplant, 1 can tomato sauce, half of oregano and half of sharp cheese. Repeat layers. Cover. **Microwave at Medium High 20 to 24 Minutes.** |
| 1 pkg. (8-oz.) ........ mozzarella cheese, sliced | Add mozzarella cheese. **Microwave at High 2 to 3 Minutes,** until cheese melts. |

Makes 4 to 6 servings

## Cheezy Broccoli

*6-oz. can water chestnuts, drained and sliced or slivered almonds can be added as option.*

POWER LEVEL: High
MICROWAVE TIME: 24 to 29 min., total

| | |
|---|---|
| 1 pkg. (10-oz.) ...... frozen chopped broccoli<br>2 tablespoons water | Place broccoli and water in 1-quart casserole. **Microwave on High 10 to 11 Minutes.** Stir after 5 minutes. Drain and set aside. |
| 1 cup packaged .... precooked (Minute) rice<br>1 can (10¾-oz.) condensed cream of chicken soup<br>½ cup milk<br>1 jar (8-oz.) pasteurized processed cheese food<br>¼ teaspoon pepper | In 1½-qt. casserole combine rice, soup, milk, cheese and pepper. **Microwave at High 2 to 4 Minutes,** until cheese melts and can be blended easily. |
| ¼ cup chopped ...... onion<br>½ cup chopped celery | To cheese mixture, add onion, celery and broccoli. Stir thoroughly. Pour into lightly greased 8-in. square dish. **Microwave at High 12 to 14 Minutes,** rotating dish ¼ turn after 5 minutes. Let stand 5 minutes before serving. |

Makes 6 servings

## Popular Green Bean Casserole

POWER LEVEL: High　　　　　　　TEMP: 170°
MICROWAVE TIME: 18 min., total

| | |
|---|---|
| 2 pkgs. (10-oz. ...... each) frozen French-style green beans | Place beans in 2-quart casserole in microwave oven. Cover. **Microwave at High 10 Minutes,** stirring once. Drain. |
| 1 can (10-oz.) ...... cream of mushroom soup<br>¼ cup milk<br>1 jar (2-oz.) pimiento, sliced and drained | Separate beans into 1½-qt. casserole. Mix with soup, milk and pimiento to blend well. |

Insert temperature probe so tip rests on center bottom of dish. Cover with plastic wrap, arranging loosely around probe to vent. Attach cable end at receptacle. **Microwave at High. Set Temp, Set 170°** When oven signals let stand, covered, about 10 minutes.

**Topping:** Arrange 1 can (3-oz.) French fried onions in a ring around edge of dish. Toss to mix, if desired.

Makes 6 to 8 servings

## Creamy Cauliflower

POWER LEVEL: High
MICROWAVE TIME: 28 to 32 min., total

| | |
|---|---|
| ½ teaspoon salt ....<br>2 tablespoons water<br>2 pkgs. (10-oz. each) frozen cauliflower | In 2-qt. casserole place salt and water. Add cauliflower. **Microwave at High 14 to 16 Minutes,** until just done. Place in strainer or colander to drain. |
| 1 tablespoon ........ butter, melted<br>1 tablespoon flour<br>½ cup milk<br>1 cup small curd cottage cheese<br>½ cup shredded cheddar cheese<br>1 tablespoon chopped pimiento<br>½ teaspoon salt<br>⅛ teaspoon pepper | In same 2-qt. casserole, stir to mix butter and flour. Stir in milk, cheeses, pimiento and seasonings. **Microwave at High 6 Minutes,** until cheese melts and mixture thickens. |
| ½ cup crushed ...... corn flakes<br>½ teaspoon paprika<br>½ teaspoon dill weed | Mix cauliflower gently into sauce and sprinkle top with corn flakes mixed with paprika and dill weed. **Microwave at High 8 to 10 Minutes,** until hot. |

Makes 6 servings

## Vegetable Lasagna

*Cook noodles (see page 13) before beginning to assemble this nutritious entree.*

POWER LEVEL: Defrost and Medium High
MICROWAVE TIME: 35 to 40 min., total.

| | |
|---|---|
| **1 pkg. (10-oz.) frozen chopped spinach** | In 8-in. square dish place unwrapped frozen block of spinach. **Microwave at Defrost 10 Minutes,** breaking apart after 6 minutes, until thawed. Squeeze dry. |
| **2 cans (8-oz. each) tomato sauce**<br>**1 can (4-oz.) sliced mushrooms, drained**<br>**¼ cup finely chopped onion**<br>**1 teaspoon oregano**<br>**½ teaspoon basil**<br>**½ teaspoon salt**<br>**¼ teaspoon garlic powder**<br>**6 lasagna noodles, cooked**<br>**1 cup small curd cottage cheese**<br>**1 pkg. (8-oz.) mozzarella cheese, shredded (2 cups)** | In small bowl mix together tomato sauce, mushrooms, onion, oregano, basil, salt and garlic powder. Spread ½ cup sauce over bottom of 8-in. square dish. Over sauce, layer half of noodles. Top with spinach, cottage cheese, half of mozzarella cheese, and half of remaining tomato sauce. Repeat noodle, sauce, and mozzarella cheese layers. **Microwave at Medium High 25 to 30 Minutes.** Let stand 5 minutes before serving. |

Makes 6 servings

## Tomato Pepper Quickie

POWER LEVEL: High
MICROWAVE TIME: 7½ to 8½ min., total

| | |
|---|---|
| **2 medium green peppers, cut into chunks**<br>**1 medium onion**<br>**½ teaspoon basil**<br>**1 teaspoon salt**<br>**2 tablespoons water** | In 1-qt. casserole place green pepper. Cut onion into ¼-in. slices, separate into rings and lay on top of green pepper. Sprinkle with seasonings. Add water. Cover. **Microwave at High 6 Minutes,** stirring after 3 minutes. |
| **2 medium ripe tomatoes or 1 can (1-lb.) tomato wedges, drained** | Cut tomatoes into ¾-in. wedges and arrange over casserole. Cover. **Microwave at High 1½ to 2½ Minutes** more, until tomatoes are just heated. |

Makes 4 servings

## Vegetable Ring

POWER LEVEL: Medium High
MICROWAVE TIME: 10 to 14 min., total

| | |
|---|---|
| **¼ cup melted butter**<br>**1 cup milk**<br>**3 eggs, well beaten**<br>**1 tablespoon grated onion**<br>**½ teaspoon salt**<br>**¼ teaspoon pepper**<br>**¾ cup cracker crumbs**<br>**1 to 1¼ cups raw or cooked vegetables (grated or mashed)** | In mixing bowl combine butter, milk, eggs, onion, salt and pepper. Beat well with fork. Stir in cracker crumbs and vegetables. Pour into well greased 5-cup glass or microwave safe plastic ring mold. **Microwave at Medium High 10 to 14 Minutes.** Rotate ¼ turn every 5 minutes. Serve in ring mold. |

Makes 4 servings.

## Tips on How to Vary Vegetables

**Pour Sauce** over cooked vegetables and toss gently to coat. For Zesty Sauce shown here, in 1-qt. casserole, mix 1 tablespoon butter and ¼ cup grated onion. Microwave at High for 3 minutes. Add 1 cup mayonnaise, ¼ cup horseradish, ½ teaspoon salt, ¼ teaspoon pepper and mix well. Pour over vegetables.

**Top Vegetables** with bacon bits, crumbled hard-boiled egg, toasted nuts, or a Butter Crumb Topping of ¼ cup melted butter, 1 cup fine bread crumbs and ¼ teaspoon dill weed or other dried herb. Microwave in a 1-qt. glass casserole at High for 2 to 3 minutes.

**Glaze** yams or other vegetables. In 1½-qt. casserole stir together ¼ cup brown sugar, 2 tablespoons butter, 1 tablespoon water and ¼ teaspoon salt. Microwave at High for 3 to 4 minutes. Stir well; add 1 pound hot, cooked vegetables. Stir gently to coat.

## Scalloped Potatoes

*If desired, sprinkle top with paprika and 1/2 cup shredded sharp cheese after cooking. Cheese melts as casserole stands.*

POWER LEVEL: High and Medium High
MICROWAVE TIME: 27 to 34 min., total

| | |
|---|---|
| **3 tablespoons butter**<br>**2 tablespoons flour**<br>**1 teaspoon salt**<br>**1/4 teaspoon pepper**<br>**2 cups milk** | Place butter in 1-qt. measuring cup. **Microwave at High 1 to 2 Minutes,** or until melted. Blend in flour and seasonings. Gradually stir in milk. **Microwave at High 8 to 10 Minutes,** stirring after 4 minutes. |
| **3½ to 4 cups thinly sliced white potatoes (about 3 medium)**<br>**2 tablespoons minced onion** | Layer half of potatoes, onion and sauce in greased 2-qt. casserole. Repeat layers. Cover. |

**Microwave at Medium High 18 to 22 Minutes.** Remove from oven and let stand 5 minutes before serving.

Makes 4 to 6 servings

## Wilted Spinach Salad

POWER LEVEL: High
MICROWAVE TIME: 6 to 10 min., total

| | |
|---|---|
| **3 strips bacon** | With scissors, snip bacon into 1-in. pieces into 2-qt. casserole. **Microwave at High 3 to 4 Minutes,** until crisp. With slotted spoon, remove bacon to paper towels to drain. |
| **1/4 cup vinegar**<br>**2 teaspoons sugar**<br>**1/4 teaspoon salt**<br>**1/8 teaspoon pepper**<br>**1/8 teaspoon crushed dried tarragon**<br>**1/4 cup chopped celery**<br>**1 tablespoon sliced green onion** | To drippings in casserole add vinegar, sugar, salt, pepper and tarragon. **Microwave at High 2 to 3 Minutes** to boil. Stir in celery and onion. |
| **6 cups torn spinach leaves, (about 1/2-lb.)**<br>**2 medium oranges, sectioned, each section seeded and cut in half\*** | Gradually add spinach to hot dressing, tossing to coat each piece, just until slightly wilted. **Microwave at High 1 to 3 Minutes** to wilt further if desired. Add orange segments and crisp bacon pieces and toss again lightly. Serve immediately. |

Makes 8 to 10 servings

*\*Or substitute 1 can (11-oz.) Mandarin oranges, drained.*

## Hot German Potato Salad

POWER LEVEL: High
MICROWAVE TIME: 21 to 27 min., total

| | |
|---|---|
| **4 medium potatoes** | Wash and pierce potatoes through with fork. Place on paper towel in microwave oven. **Microwave at High 9 to 12 Minutes,** until tender. Remove from oven, cool slightly, peel potatoes and cut in 1/8-in. slices. |
| **6 strips bacon** | In 2-qt. casserole cut bacon in small pieces. Cover with paper towel. **Microwave at High about 6 Minutes,** until crisp. With slotted spoon remove bacon to paper towels to drain. Set aside. |
| **2 tablespoons flour**<br>**1/4 cup sugar**<br>**1½ teaspoons salt**<br>**1/2 teaspoon celery seed**<br>**1/8 teaspoon pepper** | Stir flour, sugar and seasonings into bacon fat until smooth. **Microwave at High 1 to 2 Minutes,** until bubbly. |
| **1 cup water**<br>**1/2 cup vinegar** | Add water and vinegar to flour mixture. **Microwave at High 5 to 7 Minutes,** until mixture boils and thickens. Remove from oven and stir until smooth. Add potatoes and bacon; stir gently so potatoes hold their shape. Cover casserole and let stand until ready to serve. |

Makes 4 to 6 servings

## Corn Pudding

POWER LEVEL: Medium High
MICROWAVE TIME: 15 to 16 min., total

| | |
|---|---|
| **1 egg**<br>**1/2 cup milk**<br>**1 tablespoon sugar**<br>**1 can (17-oz.) cream style corn**<br>**3/4 cup crushed crackers**<br>**2 tablespoons butter, cut in pieces** | Place egg in 1½-qt. casserole and beat well with fork. Stir in milk, sugar, corn, crackers and butter. Cover. **Microwave at Medium High 10 Minutes** and stir well. |
| **paprika** | Sprinkle with paprika. Cover. **Microwave at Medium High 5 to 6 Minutes.** When done, center will be just barely set. |

Makes 4 servings

## Stir Fry Vegetables

POWER LEVEL: High
MICROWAVE TIME: 12 to 14 min., total

| | |
|---|---|
| 1 tablespoon oil . . . .<br>1 tablespoon butter<br>2 medium onions,<br>    quartered<br>    lengthwise | In 2-qt. glass casserole place oil, butter and onions. **Microwave uncovered at High for 4 Minutes** until hot. |
| 1 small green<br>    pepper, cut in ¼-in.<br>    wide strips<br>1 cup carrots<br>    (3 medium),<br>    diagonally sliced<br>1 cup broccoli<br>    flowerets<br>1 cup cauliflower<br>    flowerets<br>1 stalk celery,<br>    diagonally sliced | Stir in and mix well green pepper, carrots, broccoli, cauliflower and celery. **Microwave at High, covered, for 4 Minutes.** |
| ½ cup thinly-sliced . .<br>    cooked meat<br>½ cup sliced<br>    mushrooms | Add meat and mushrooms and continue to **Microwave at High uncovered for 4 to 6 Minutes** more. |

Makes 6 to 8 servings

*Stir Fry Vegetables*

## Creamed Vegetables

POWER LEVEL: High
MICROWAVE TIME: 5 to 6½ min., total

| | |
|---|---|
| 2 tablespoons butter . .<br>2 tablespoons flour<br>½ teaspoon salt | In 1½-qt. glass casserole place butter, flour and salt. **Microwave at High for 1 to 1½ Minutes,** whisking well. |
| 1¼ cups milk or . . . . . .<br>    Half & Half | Gradually stir in milk. **Microwave at High for 4 to 5 Minutes,** stirring every minute until thick and bubbly. Covers 1 to 2 pounds cooked vegetables. |

Makes 1¼ cups sauce

## Zippy Zucchini

POWER LEVEL: High and Medium
MICROWAVE TIME: 18 to 20 min., total

| | |
|---|---|
| 4 cups zucchini, . . . .<br>    cut into chunks<br>    (2 medium)<br>½ medium onion,<br>    thinly sliced | Place zucchini and onion in 8-in round dish. Cover with plastic wrap, turning one edge back slightly to vent. **Microwave at High 12 Minutes.** Drain. |
| 4 eggs, beaten . . . . . .<br>1½ cups (6-oz.)<br>    shredded cheddar<br>    cheese<br>1 jar (2-oz.) pimiento,<br>    drained<br>½ teaspoon salt<br>⅛ teaspoon pepper | In large bowl mix together eggs, cheese, pimiento, salt and pepper. Add zucchini and onions, stirring well. Grease dish in which vegetables were cooked. Pour mixture into dish and cover with plastic wrap. **Microwave at Medium 3 Minutes.** Stir cooked edges to center, then cover and **Microwave at Medium 4 to 5 Minutes,** until center is set. |

Makes 4 to 6 servings

## Frozen Vegetable Cooking Chart

POWER LEVEL: High

1. In 1-qt. casserole place 2 tablespoons of water and ½ teaspoon salt. Add a 10-oz. package of frozen vegetable. Cover. Stir or rearrange after half of cooking time.

| Vegetable | Time | Comments |
|---|---|---|
| Broccoli, Chopped | 10 to 11 min. | |
|       Spears | 10 to 11 min. | |
| Cauliflower, Floweretes | 9 to 10 min. | Do not cover. |
| Corn, Kernal | 7 to 9 min. | Do not cover. |
| Peas, Shelled | 6 to 7 min. | |
| Spinach, Chopped | 8 to 9 min. | Use 3 tablespoons water. |
| Vegetables, Mixed | 10 to 11 min. | Use 3 tablespoons water. |

## Bran Nut Muffins

POWER LEVEL: Medium High
MICROWAVE TIME: See chart below

| | |
|---|---|
| **1½ cups unsifted** . . . .<br>  **all-purpose flour**<br>**1 cup sugar**<br>**5 teaspoons baking**<br>  **powder**<br>**1½ teaspoons salt**<br>**2 cups whole bran**<br>  **cereal**<br>**1 cup chopped nuts**<br>  **or raisins** | In large mixing bowl stir together flour, sugar, baking powder, salt, bran and nuts or raisins. |
| **2 eggs** . . . . . . . . . . . .<br>**1½ cups milk**<br>**½ cup cooking oil** | Combine eggs, milk and oil. Stir into dry mixture just until all flour is dampened. Fill paper lined muffin cups ½ full. |
| **¼ cup crushed** . . . . .<br>  **bran cereal or**<br>  **chopped**<br>  **nuts** | Sprinkle muffins with cereal or nuts. **Microwave at Medium High,** using chart below. |

Makes about 24 muffins

## Muffin Cooking Chart

POWER LEVEL: Medium High

| Muffins | Time | Comments |
|---|---|---|
| 1 Muffin | ¾ to 1¼ min. | Use microwave muffin container or homemade muffin cups (made by cutting down hot drink cups). Check for doneness at minimum time. Rich, thick batters may take longest time. |
| 2 to 4: | 1 to 3 min. | |
| 5 to 6: | 3 to 4½ min. | |

## Everyday Coffee Cake

POWER LEVEL: Medium High
MICROWAVE TIME: 6½ to 8 min., total

| | |
|---|---|
| **1½ cups buttermilk** . .<br>  **biscuit mix**<br>**¼ cup sugar** | In mixing bowl stir together biscuit mix and sugar. |
| **½ cup milk** . . . . . . . . .<br>**1 egg**<br>**2 tablespoons**<br>  **cooking oil** | Add milk, egg and oil. Beat by hand, mixing well. Pour into greased 8-in. round dish. |
| **⅓ cup buttermilk** . . . .<br>  **biscuit mix**<br>**⅓ cup brown sugar**<br>  **(packed)**<br>**2 tablespoons butter**<br>**1 teaspoon**<br>  **cinnamon**<br>**¼ cup chopped nuts** | Blend biscuit mix, brown sugar, butter and cinnamon until crumbly. Sprinkle over batter and sprinkle with nuts. **Microwave at Medium High 6½ to 8 Minutes.** Rotate ¼ turn after 4 minutes. Cool 15 minutes; drizzle with Fine Glaze. Serve warm. |

**Fine Glaze:** Stir together ¾ cup confectioners sugar and 1 tablespoon milk. From tip of spoon, drizzle glaze over cake in spoke fashion.

Makes 1 (8-in. round) cake

## Cornbread Ring

POWER LEVEL: Medium High
MICROWAVE TIME: 8 to 9 min., total

| | |
|---|---|
| **1 cup yellow** . . . . . . .<br>  **corn meal**<br>**1 cup unsifted**<br>  **all-purpose flour**<br>**2 tablespoons sugar**<br>**4 teaspoons baking**<br>  **powder**<br>**¾ teaspoon salt** | In large mixing bowl, stir together cornmeal, flour, sugar, baking powder and salt. |
| **1 egg** . . . . . . . . . . . . .<br>**1 cup milk**<br>**½ cup cooking oil** | Add egg, milk and cooking oil. Beat until smooth, about 1 minute. |
| **1 can finely** . . . . . .<br>  **crushed French**<br>  **fried onions**<br>  **(2.8-oz. can)**<br>**2 tablespoons**<br>  **Parmesan cheese** | Place onions and cheese in well-greased 2-quart ring mold. Tilt to coat bottom and sides. Pour batter into ring mold. |

**Microwave at Medium High for 8 to 9 Minutes** until toothpick inserted in center comes out clean. Rotate ¼ turn after 4 minutes. Let stand 5 minutes. Turn out on cooling rack or serving plate. Serve warm.

Makes 1 (8-in.) ring

**Coffee cakes** may be microwaved in a round dish, rather than a ring. The richer, sweeter batter cooks evenly, so there will be no depression in the center. Like other quick breads, coffee cakes do not brown, and need a colorful topping or simple icing to give them a finished appearance.

## Cherry Caramel Ring

POWER LEVEL: High and Medium
MICROWAVE TIME: 7 to 9 min., total

| | |
|---|---|
| **¼ cup butter** . . . . . . . . | Place butter in 8-in. round dish. **Microwave at High 1 to 1½ Minutes,** until melted. |
| **½ cup brown sugar** . .<br>  **(packed)**<br>**2 tablespoons light**<br>  **corn syrup**<br>**½ cup pecan halves**<br>**¼ cup maraschino**<br>  **cherries, quartered** | Sprinkle sugar over butter and add corn syrup. Stir well with fork. Place drinking glass open-side-up in center of dish. Sprinkle with pecans and cherries. |
| **1 roll (10-oz.)** . . . . . . . .<br>  **refrigerated**<br>  **buttermilk biscuits** | Arrange biscuits over mixture in dish in petal shape, squeezing to fit, if necessary. **Microwave at Medium 6 to 7 Minutes.** Remove glass and invert onto serving plate. Let dish stand over rolls a few minutes so remaining syrup in dish may drizzle over rolls. Serve warm. |

Makes 1 (8-in.) ring

## Fluffy Marshmallow Fruit Pie

*Pie is creamy and soft when served from refrigerator. For firm pieces which hold sharp cut, serve frozen. Frozen pie releases easily from bottom of pie plate if set on a towel dampened with hot water for a few minutes.*

**POWER LEVEL:** High
**MICROWAVE TIME:** 3 to 4 min., total

| | |
|---|---|
| **Crumb Pie Shell (below)** .. | Microwave Crumb Pie Shell using the flavor of cookie that best complements filling. Cool. |
| **1 pkg. (10-oz.)** ...... **large marshmallows** **½ cup milk** | In 2-qt. casserole place marshmallows and milk. Cover. **Microwave at High 3 to 4 Minutes,** until mixture can be stirred smooth. Chill in refrigerator (about 30 to 40 minutes) or in pan of ice water, until thickened, stirring occasionally. |
| **1 cup whipping** ...... **cream, whipped** **2 cups fresh fruit** | Fold in whipped cream and peeled and sliced fresh peaches, sliced fresh strawberries or fresh whole raspberries. Pour into crust and decorate with reserved crumbs or additional whipped cream, if desired. Refrigerate several hours or overnight. |

Makes 1 (9-in.) pie

## Frozen Chocolate Almond Pie

*This pie cuts well straight from the freezer. No thawing is necessary. Use wet knife for sharpest cut. Also see tip with above recipe.*

**POWER LEVEL:** High
**MICROWAVE TIME:** 4 min., total

| | |
|---|---|
| **Crumb Pie Shell** .. **(below)** | Microwave pie shell. Cool. |
| **4 milk chocolate** .... **candy bars with almonds (1.15-oz. each)** **½ of 10-oz. pkg. large marshmallows (about 25)** **½ cup milk** | In 2-qt. casserole place candy, marshmallows and milk. **Microwave at High 4 Minutes,** stirring after 2 minutes, until mixture can be stirred smooth. Chill until thickened, stirring occasionally. |
| **1 cup whipping** ...... **cream, whipped** | Fold whipped cream into cooled chocolate mixture. Pile into pie shell and freeze until firm. |

Makes 1 (9-in.) pie

## Crumb Pie Shell

Crumb crusts can be made with a variety of cookie crumbs. Mix ¼ cup melted butter, 1¼ cups crumbs, 2 tablespoons sugar. Press into a 9-in. pie plate.
**Microwave at High 2 to 3 Minutes.**

## Apple Graham Pie

**POWER LEVEL:** High
**MICROWAVE TIME:** 17½ to 19½ min., total

| | |
|---|---|
| **½ cup (¼-lb.)** ....... **butter** **¼ cup sugar** **2 cups graham cracker crumbs** | In large glass mixing bowl place butter. **Microwave at High 2½ Minutes,** until melted. Add sugar and crumbs. Mix well. Press half of mixture firmly and evenly into 9-in. pie plate. |
| **5 cups thinly** ....... **sliced (4 to 6 medium)** **½ cup sugar** **1 teaspoon cinnamon** | In large mixing bowl place apples slices. Add sugar and cinnamon, mixing well. Mound and press down into crumb crust. |

Cover apples with remaining crumbs to make top crust. Press crumbs down firmly, especially at edges, to prevent boilover.

**Microwave at High 15 to 17 Minutes.** Rotate ¼ turn after 8 minutes. Let stand 10 minutes.

Makes 1 (9-in.) pie

## Pumpkin Pie

**POWER LEVEL:** High and Medium
**MICROWAVE TIME:** 37 to 39 min., total

| | |
|---|---|
| **½ cup (¼-lb.)** ....... **butter** | In 10-in. pie plate place butter. **Microwave at High 2½ Minutes,** until melted. |
| **2 cups vanilla** ...... **wafer crumbs** **2 tablespoons sugar** | Add crumbs and sugar; mix well. Firmly press on bottom and up sides of dish. **Microwave at High 4 Minutes,** rotating dish ¼ turn every minute. |
| **1 can (16-oz.)** ....... **pumpkin** **1 cup brown sugar (packed)** **1 tablespoon pumpkin pie spice** **1 tablespoon flour** **½ teaspoon salt** **1 can (13-oz.) evaporated milk** **2 eggs, beaten** | In 2-qt. casserole blend together pumpkin, brown sugar, pumpkin pie spice, flour, salt, evaporated milk and eggs. **Microwave at Medium 15 Minutes,** stirring every 5 minutes, until hot and thickened. |
| | Pour hot filling into prepared pie shell. **Microwave at Medium 15 to 17 Minutes.** Pie is done when edges are set and center is slightly soft. Let stand about 30 minutes. |

Makes 1 (10-in.) pie

# Pies and Cakes

## Basic Pastry Shell

POWER LEVEL: High
MICROWAVE TIME: 6 to 7 min., total

| | |
|---|---|
| **1 cup unsifted** . . . . . . **all-purpose flour** <br> **1 teaspoon salt** <br> **6 tablespoons shortening** | In small bowl place flour and salt. With pastry blender cut in shortening, until mixture resembles the size of small peas. |
| **2 to 3 tablespoons** . . **cold water** | Sprinkle water over flour-shortening mixture. Stir with fork to form ball. |

Roll out on floured pastry cloth with rolling pin to ⅛-in. thickness. Let stand a few minutes before shaping. Use to line 9-in. pie plate shaping pastry to the edge of pie plate. Prick pastry with fork. **Microwave at High 6 to 7 Minutes.**

Makes 1 (9-in.) pastry shell

### Chocolate Pastry Shell Variation:
To flour add only ½ teaspoon salt along with 2 tablespoons cocoa and ⅓ cup sugar.

## Popular Carrot Cake

POWER LEVEL: Low and High
MICROWAVE TIME: 18 to 20 min., total

| | |
|---|---|
| **1¼ cups sugar** . . . . . . . <br> **1 cup cooking oil** <br> **1 teaspoon vanilla extract** <br> **3 eggs** | In large mixing bowl blend sugar, oil and vanilla. Add eggs and beat well. |
| **1½ cups unsifted** . . . . **all-purpose flour** <br> **¾ teaspoon salt** <br> **1½ teaspoons baking soda** <br> **2½ teaspoons cinnamon** | In small bowl, stir together flour, salt, soda and cinnamon. Add to sugar-egg mixture and mix in. |
| **2¼ cups grated raw** . . **carrots** <br> **½ cup chopped walnuts** | Fold in carrots and walnuts. Pour batter into 16-cup plastic microwave fluted or striaght-sided ring mold. |

**Microwave at Low 10 Minutes,** then at **High 8 to 10 Minutes,** rotating dish ¼ turn every 5 minutes. Let stand directly on heat-proof counter or wooden board 10 minutes before inverting. Glaze with Cream Cheese Glaze, below, if desired.

Makes 1 (10-in.) tube cake

## Cream Cheese Glaze

POWER LEVEL: HIGH
MICROWAVE TIME: ¼ to ½ min., total

| | |
|---|---|
| **1 (3-oz.) pkg.** . . . . . . . . **cream cheese** <br> **½ cup confectioners sugar** <br> **3 tablespoons butter** <br> **1½ tablespoons milk** <br> **1 teaspoon vanilla extract** | In small glass mixing bowl, place cheese. **Microwave at High ¼ to ½ Minute,** just to soften. Add sugar, butter milk and vanilla. Beat with mixer until smooth. |

## Quiche Pastry

*The butter flavor complements quiche. See Classic Quiche Lorraine page 33.*

POWER LEVEL: High
MICROWAVE TIME: 5 to 7 min., total

| | |
|---|---|
| **1 cup unsifted** . . . . . . **all-purpose flour** <br> **½ teaspoon salt** <br> **3 tablespoons shortening** <br> **3 tablespoons cold butter** | In small mixing bowl stir together flour and salt. With pastry blender, cut in shortening until it has the appearance of cornmeal. Cut in butter until particles form the size of peas. |
| **2½ tablespoons** . . . . . . **cold water** | Sprinkle mixture with cold water. Blend lightly with fingers until dough holds together and can be formed into ball. Roll out to fit 9-in quiche dish. |
| **1 egg yolk** . . . . . . . . . <br> **1 teaspoon Worcestershire sauce** | Brush pastry with mixture of egg yolk and Worcestershire sauce. |

**Microwave at High 5 to 7 Minutes.** Rotate dish and press down any air bubbles after 4 minutes.

Makes 1 (9-in.) quiche pastry

## Honey Drizzle Cake

*This recipe won $5,000 in a microwave recipe contest. The syrup is plentiful, and some people prefer to use only half of it to soak into cake.*

POWER LEVEL: Medium High and High
MICROWAVE TIME: 19 to 22 min., total

| | |
|---|---|
| **5 eggs** . . . . . . . . . . . . . <br> **¼ cup sugar** <br> **⅛ teaspoon salt** | Separate eggs. In large mixer bowl beat egg whites until foamy. Gradually beat in ¼ cup sugar and salt until fluffy. |
| **½ cup sugar** . . . . . . . . <br> **1 teaspoon vanilla extract** | In small bowl beat egg yolks, ½ cup sugar and vanilla until thick and pale. |
| **1½ cups chopped** . . . . **pecans** <br> **1½ cups fine vanilla wafer crumbs** <br> **1½ teaspoons baking powder** <br> **½ teaspoon cinnamon** | Fold yolk mixture into egg whites thoroughly. Blend pecans, wafer crumbs, baking powder and cinnamon; sprinkle over top. Fold all ingredients together well. |

Pour into greased 8-in. square dish. Cover with wax paper, **Microwave at Medium High 9 to 10 Minutes.** Rotate ¼ turn every 3 minutes. Remove cake and cook Honey Syrup (below). Carefully pour ⅔ of syrup over cake. Serve in small pieces, warm or cold, with unsweetened whipped cream and remaining syrup.

**Honey Syrup:** In 2-qt. casserole stir together 1½ cups water, 1½ cups sugar and ⅔ cup honey. **Microwave at High 10 to 12 Minutes,** stirring after 4 minutes.

Makes 1 (8-in.) square cake

## Basic Butter Cake

POWER LEVEL: High
MICROWAVE TIME: 8 to 9 min., per layer

| | |
|---|---|
| 2 cups unsifted all-purpose flour<br>2 cups sugar<br>1 tablespoon baking powder<br>½ teaspoon salt | In large mixing bowl stir together flour, sugar, baking powder and salt. |
| 1 cup (½-lb.) butter, softened<br>1 cup milk<br>1½ teaspoons vanilla extract<br>1 egg | Add butter, milk, vanilla and 1 egg. Beat 2 minutes at lowest speed of mixer, scraping bowl constantly for first ½ minute. |
| 3 eggs | Stop mixer and add eggs. Continue beating at lowest speed, scraping bowl often, 1 more minute. Batter will look curdled. |

Pour batter into 2 wax paper lined 8-in. round dishes: spread evenly. Microwave 1 cake at a time. **Microwave at High 8 to 9 Minutes.** Rotate ½ turn after 4 minutes. Let stand directly on heat-proof counter or wooden board to cool 15 minutes. Cake may then be turned out on wire rack to complete cooling, if desired.

Makes 2 (8-in.) round cakes

## Pineapple Upside Down Cake

*For variety substitute peaches for pineapple and almond extract for vanilla.*

POWER LEVEL: High and Medium High
MICROWAVE TIME: 13 to 14 min., total

| | |
|---|---|
| ¼ cup butter<br>⅓ cup brown sugar (packed)<br>1 can (8¼-oz.) pineapple slices<br>4 maraschino or candied cherries, cut in half | In 8-in. round dish place butter. **Microwave at High 1 to 1½ Minutes,** to melt. Sprinkle sugar over butter. Drain pineapple (save liquid) on paper towels and arrange in dish. Decorate with cherries. |
| 1¼ cups unsifted all-purpose flour<br>¾ cup sugar<br>2 teaspoons baking powder<br>½ teaspoon salt<br>⅓ cup soft shortening<br>1 egg<br>Liquid from pineapple plus milk to total ½ cup<br>1 teaspoon vanilla extract | In small mixer bowl place flour, sugar, baking powder, salt, shortening, egg, liquid and vanilla. Beat 3 minutes on lowest mixer speed, scraping bowl constantly first ½ minute. Carefully spread batter over fruit in dish. **Microwave at Medium High 12 to 13 Minutes.** Some batter may run onto edges of dish, but will not spill. When done, toothpick stuck in cake comes out clean. Invert cake onto plate, let dish stand over cake a few minutes. Serve warm. |

Makes 1 (8-in.) round cake

## Basic Cheesecake

POWER LEVEL: High and Low
MICROWAVE TIME: 17 to 21½ min., total

| | |
|---|---|
| 3 tablespoons butter<br>1 cup fine crumbs (graham cracker or chocolate cookie)<br>2 tablespoons sugar | In 8-in. round dish place butter. **Microwave at High 1¼ to 1½ Minutes,** to melt. Stir in crumbs and sugar. Press mixture on bottom and sides of dish. **Microwave at High 3 to 4 Minutes,** rotating dish ½ turn after 1 minute, until set. |
| 4 eggs<br>1 cup sugar<br>2 pkgs. (8-oz. each) cream cheese<br>2 teaspoons vanilla extract<br>¼ teaspoon salt | In blender container place eggs, sugar, cream cheese, vanilla and salt. Blend on high speed 1 minute until smooth. (If mixed with electric mixer, use large mixer bowl and mix at high speed 3 minutes.) Pour into bowl. **Microwave at High 5 to 6 Minutes** until hot, whisking every minute until smooth. Pour over back of spoon into crust. |

**Microwave at Low 8 to 10 Minutes,** until center is almost set. Rotate ¼ turn after 5 minutes. Refrigerate at least 3 hours before serving. Garnish with Whipped Cream Cheese Topping (below) and chocolate curls, if desired.

Makes 1 (8-in.) cheesecake

**Whipped Cream Cheese Topping:** In small mixer bowl place 1 pkg. (3-oz.) softened cream cheese, ½ cup whipping cream and 2 tablespoons sugar. Beat until fluffy. Serve in dollops or spread over top.

## Chocolate Chip Filled Cupcakes

| | |
|---|---|
| Batter from 2-layer chocolate cake mix<br>Chocolate Chip Filling (below) | To make each cupcake, measure about 1 tablespoon batter into paper liner. Cover with 1 rounded teaspoon filling. Top with 1 more tablespoon of batter. |

Microwave cupcakes using chart below. As cupcakes cook, filling will form in center.

**Chocolate Chip Filling:** Stir together 1 pkg. (8-oz.) softened cream cheese, ⅓ cup sugar, 1 egg, ⅛ teaspoon salt, until well mixed. Blend in 1 cup (6-oz.) miniature chocolate chips.

Makes 30 cupcakes

POWER LEVEL: Medium High

| CUPCAKES | TIME MINUTES | COMMENTS |
|---|---|---|
| 2 to 4 | 2 to 3½ | Fill paper liners only half full. Check at minimum time. |
| 5 to 6 | 3 to 4½ | |

## Streuseled Apples

POWER LEVEL: High
MICROWAVE TIME: 15 to 17 min., total

| | |
|---|---|
| **6 cups sliced,** ...... **peeled apples**<br>**¾ cup brown sugar (packed)** | In 8-in. square dish place apples and sugar. |
| **½ cup unsifted** ...... **all-purpose flour**<br>**⅓ cup brown sugar (packed)**<br>**⅓ cup quick-cooking oats**<br>**½ cup (¼-lb.) butter**<br>**½ teaspoon cinnamon** | With pastry blender mix flour, sugar, oats, butter and cinnamon until crumbly. Sprinkle over top of apples. |

**Microwave at High 15 to 17 Minutes.** Let stand a few minutes before serving.

Makes 6 to 8 servings

## Butterscotch Bananas

POWER LEVEL: High
MICROWAVE TIME: 5 to 7 min., total

| | |
|---|---|
| **½ cup brown sugar** .. **(packed)**<br>**¼ cup rum**<br>**¼ cup butter** | In 1½-qt. casserole stir together brown sugar and rum. Add butter. Cover. **Microwave at High 4 to 5 Minutes,** until sugar is dissolved. |
| **2 large ripe, firm** .... **bananas** | Cut bananas lengthwise, then crosswise so there are 8 pieces. Add to syrup, stirring to coat each piece. **Microwave at High 1 to 2 Minutes,** until hot. Serve over ice cream. |

Makes 4 servings

## Basic Brownies

POWER LEVEL: High
MICROWAVE TIME: 6 to 7½ min., total

| | |
|---|---|
| **2 eggs** .............<br>**1 cup sugar**<br>**½ teaspoon salt**<br>**1 teaspoon vanilla extract** | In small bowl at medium speed on mixer, beat together eggs, sugar, salt and vanilla, about 1 minute until light. |
| **½ cup (⅓-lb.)** ....... **butter, melted** | Add melted butter. Continue beating until thoroughly blended. |
| **¾ cup unsifted all-** .. **purpose flour**<br>**½ cup cocoa** | Mix in flour and cocoa at low speed. |
| **1 cup chopped** ...... **nuts** | Stir in nuts. Spread evenly in greased 8-in. square dish. |

**Microwave at High 6 to 7½ Minutes,** rotating dish ½ turn after 3 minutes. When done, top looks shiny but dry and will spring back when lightly touched. Cut when cold.

Makes about 20 brownies

## Chocolate Chip Bars

POWER LEVEL: Medium High
MICROWAVE TIME: 10 to 12 min., total

| | |
|---|---|
| **½ cup (¼-lb.)** ........ **butter, softened**<br>**¾ cup brown sugar (packed)**<br>**1 egg**<br>**1 tablespoon milk**<br>**1 teaspoon vanilla extract** | In small mixer bowl cream together butter and sugar, until fluffy. Add egg, milk, and vanilla. Mix well. |
| **1¼ cups unsifted** .... **all-purpose flour**<br>**½ teaspoon baking powder**<br>**⅛ teaspoon salt**<br>**1 cup (6-oz.) semi-sweet chocolate pieces, divided**<br>**½ cup chopped nuts (optional)** | Stir together flour, baking powder and salt. Add to creamed mixture. Blend well. Stir in ½ cup chocolate pieces and nuts. Spread in greased 8-in. square dish. Sprinkle with remaining ½ cup chocolate pieces. Elevate dish on trivet or inverted pie plate, **Microwave at Medium High 10 to 12 Minutes,** rotating dish ½ turn every 5 minutes, until done. Cool and cut into bars. |

Makes about 24 bars

## Raspberry Tart Squares

POWER LEVEL: High and Medium
MICROWAVE TIME: 16 to 19 min., total

| | |
|---|---|
| **½ cup (¼ lb.) butter** ..<br>**¾ cup brown sugar (packed)**<br>**1 cup unsifted all-purpose flour**<br>**½ teaspoon baking powder**<br>**¼ teaspoon salt**<br>**1 cup quick-cooking oatmeal**<br>**½ cup finely chopped pecans** | In 8-in. square dish, place butter. Cover. **Microwave at High 1 to 2 Minutes,** until melted. Stir in brown sugar, flour, baking powder, salt, oatmeal and pecans; blend well. Remove 1½ cups of crumb mixture to bowl or wax paper. Pat remaining crumbs evenly over bottom of dish. Elevate dish on trivet. **Microwave at Medium 7 Minutes,** rotating dish ½ turn after 4 minutes. Cool slightly. |
| **¾ cup raspberry** .... **jam** | Cover patted-out crumbs with raspberry jam and sprinkle remaining crumbs over top. |

Place dish on trivet. **Microwave at Medium 8 to 10 Minutes,** rotating dish ½ turn after 5 minutes. Cool completely before cutting.

Makes about 16 squares

## Cinnamon Sugar Sauce

POWER LEVEL: High
MICROWAVE TIME: 4 to 5 min., total

| ½ cup sugar ........ | In 1-qt. casserole stir |
| 1½ tablespoons cornstarch | together sugar, cornstarch, cinnamon and water until completely smooth. Cover. |
| 1 teaspoon cinnamon | **Microwave at High 4** |
| 1 cup hot tap water | **to 5 Minutes,** stirring sauce after 1½ minutes. |
| 2 tablespoons ...... butter | Stir in butter until well blended. Serve warm. |

Makes 1⅓ cups

### Lemon Sauce Variation:
Prepare recipe for Cinnamon Sugar Sauce, omitting cinnamon. Stir 1 tablespoon lemon juice and 1 to 2 teaspoons finely grated lemon peel into sugar mixture.

## Scrumptious Butterscotch Sauce

POWER LEVEL: High
MICROWAVE TIME: 6 to 8 min., total

| 1 tablespoon ........ cornstarch | In 1½-qt. casserole stir together cornstarch and brown sugar. Stir in half & half, corn syrup and salt. Add butter. Cover. |
| 1¼ cups light brown sugar (packed) | |
| ½ cup dairy half & half | **Microwave at High 6** |
| 2 tablespoons light corn syrup | **to 8 Minutes,** stirring after 2 minutes, until thickened and sugar is dissolved. |
| ⅛ teaspoon salt | |
| ¼ cup butter | |
| 1 teaspoon vanilla .. extract | Add vanilla and stir until smooth and well blended. Serve warm or cold. |

Makes 1½ cups

**Fudge Sauce:** In 2-qt. dish mix 1 cup sugar, ¼ teaspoon salt and 1 can (5.3-oz.) evaporated milk. Microwave at High for 6 to 8 minutes until boiling. Stir once. Stir in 2 squares (2-oz.) unsweetened chocolate until melted. Add 2 tablespoons butter and 1 teaspoon vanilla extract.

**Marshmallow Cream Sauce:** In glass or ceramic bowl mix 2 tablespoons milk and 2 jars (7-oz. each) marshmallow creme. Microwave at Medium for 2 to 3 minutes. Stir well. Good on chocolate ice cream.

**Cherries Jubilee:** Into 2-qt. dish drain juice from 2 cans (16-oz. each) dark sweet cherries. Stir in 3 tablespoons cornstarch, 1 tablespoon lemon juice, 1 teaspoon grated lemon peel and ¾ cup sugar. Microwave at High 7 to 10 minutes, stirring after 5 minutes. Add cherries.

**Toasted Coconut:** Spread 1 cup coconut (4-oz. can) in thin layer in glass pie plate. Microwave at High for 6 to 8 minutes, stirring every minute. Serve over pie, pudding, or frosted cake.

**Mint Sauce:** Place 1 package (6½-oz.) chocolate-covered mint patties in 1-qt. glass measure with ¼ cup whipping cream. Microwave at Medium for 2 to 3 minutes. Good on mint ice cream or angel food cake.

**Dessert Fondue:** Prepare Fudge Sauce (above) or Butterscotch Sauce (above); thin with brandy, rum or liqueur if desired. Pour into fondue pot. Dip banana slices, maraschino cherries, pineapple chunks and other fruits, or angel food or pound cake pieces.

**S'Mores:** On paper plate or napkin place graham cracker square. Top with square of chocolate bar and 1 marshmallow. Microwave at Medium High 30 seconds.

**Caramel Apples:** In 1-pt. measure place half of 14-oz. pkg. unwrapped caramels with 1 tablespoon water. Microwave at High 2 to 2½ minutes. Stir until smooth. Insert wooden sticks into stem ends of 4 apples for dipping.

**Marshmallow Crisp:** In 8-in. square dish melt ¼ cup butter at High 1 minute. Add 10-oz. pkg. marshmallows; cover. Microwave at High for 4 minutes. Stir. Add 4 cups crispy rice cereal. Blend and press firmly into pan.

## Munching Peanut Brittle

POWER LEVEL:  High
MICROWAVE TIME:  12 to 14 min., total

| | |
|---|---|
| **1 cup sugar** . . . . . . . . . . <br> **½ cup white corn syrup** | In 1½-qt. casserole stir together sugar and syrup. **Microwave at High 4 Minutes.** |
| **1 cup roasted,** . . . . . . <br> **salted peanuts** | Stir in peanuts. **Microwave at High 7 to 9 Minutes.** Stir well, then continue to cook 1 to 2 minutes until peanuts are light brown. |
| **1 teaspoon butter** . . <br> **1 teaspoon vanilla extract** | Add butter and vanilla to syrup, blending well. **Microwave at High 1 Minute more.** Peanuts will be lightly browned and syrup very hot. |
| **1 teaspoon baking** . . <br> **soda** | Add baking soda and gently stir until light and foamy. |

Pour mixture onto lightly greased cookie sheet, or unbuttered non-stick coated cookie sheet. Let cool ½ to 1 hour. When cool, break into small pieces and store in air-tight container.

Makes about 1 pound

## How to Melt Chocolate

**Chocolate Bits:** Cover dish of bits with plastic wrap and Microwave at Medium. For 6-oz. pkg. (1 cup) Microwave 4 minutes until bits are glossy but hold their shape. For 12-oz. pkg., microwave 6 minutes.

**Caramel Popcorn:** In 2-qt. dish place 1-lb. box brown sugar, ½ cup butter, ½ cup light corn syrup, 1 tablespoon water and 1 teaspoon salt. Microwave at High 15 minutes, stirring after 6 minutes. Add 2 teaspoons baking soda. Pour over 3 quarts popcorn and 1 cup peanuts; toss. Spread on foil to cool or form into balls.

**3-Minute Fudge:** Stir together 1-lb. box confectioners sugar, ½ cup cocoa, ¼ teaspoon salt, ¼ cup milk and 1 tablespoon vanilla extract until blended in 1½-qt. dish. Top with ½ cup butter. Microwave at High 3 minutes. Stir smooth. Blend in 1 cup chopped nuts. Pour into wax paper lined 8-in. square dish. Chill.

**Chocolate Nut Bark:** Melt 12-oz. pkg. semi-sweet chocolate bits as shown above. Stir in 1 cup whole toasted almonds. Spread thinly over waxed paper covered cardboard, or cookie sheet. Chill until firm. Break into pieces.

# INDEX

Printed in Japan
**(4F0AG)** 86. 3 ㉚